How Organizations Develop Activists

How Organizations Develop Activists

Civic Associations and Leadership in the 21st Century

HAHRIE HAN

OXFORD
UNIVERSITY PRESS

UNIVERSITY PRESS

Oxford University Press is a department of the University of Oxford.
It furthers the University's objective of excellence in research,
scholarship, and education by publishing worldwide.

Oxford   New York
Auckland   Cape Town   Dar es Salaam   Hong Kong   Karachi
Kuala Lumpur   Madrid   Melbourne   Mexico City   Nairobi
New Delhi   Shanghai   Taipei   Toronto

With offices in
Argentina   Austria   Brazil   Chile   Czech Republic   France   Greece
Guatemala   Hungary   Italy   Japan   Poland   Portugal   Singapore
South Korea   Switzerland   Thailand   Turkey   Ukraine   Vietnam

Oxford is a registered trademark of Oxford University Press
in the UK and certain other countries.

Published in the United States of America by
Oxford University Press
198 Madison Avenue, New York, NY 10016

Library of Congress Cataloging-in-Publication Data
Han, Hahrie.
How organizations develop activists : civic associations and leadership in
the 21st century / Hahrie Han.
pages cm
Includes bibliographical references and index.
ISBN 978-0-19-933676-0 (hardback)—ISBN 978-0-19-933677-7 (paperback)
1. Public interest groups—United States—Management   2. Public interest groups—
United States—Membership.   3. Pressure groups—United States—Management.
4. Pressure groups—United States—Membership.   5. Political leadership—United States.
I. Title.
JK1118.H348 2014
322.4068—dc23
2014002901

9 8 7 6 5 4 3 2 1
Printed in the United States of America
on acid-free paper

For Kaya, Kaeson, and Jaemin

CONTENTS

LIST OF TABLES AND FIGURES

ACKNOWLEDGMENTS

This book benefited from the participation, wisdom, and support of many people. First and foremost, I should thank all the people in People for the Environment and the National Association of Doctors who graciously let me into their worlds. With humor and good cheer, they gave me rides, put me on their email lists, incorporated me into their meetings, participated in interviews, and introduced me to other people in the organization. They made the work fun and taught me an enormous amount along the way. I began this project because of my belief in the possibilities of American civic life; after having spent time with the volunteers and leaders in the study for two years, I finish this project with a strengthened sense of hope.

I should also thank the many friends and colleagues who gave me feedback on the project by reading drafts, responding to talks, and participating in conferences where I presented the work. Some responded to embarrassingly early drafts with charity and insight. The book is (hopefully) much improved as a result of everyone's feedback, and of course all the errors that remain are mine alone. This list includes Matt Baggetta, Jason Barabas, Jeff Berry, Jane Booth-Tobin, Tom Burke, Andrea Campbell, Joy Cushman, Milan DeVries, Jamie Druckman, Archon Fung, Marshall Ganz, Kristin Goss, Don Green, Michael Heaney, Dave Karpf, Taeku Lee, Matt Levendusky, Susan Moffitt, Jenny Oser, Patricia Strach, Dara Strolovitch, Lily Tsai, Ed Walker, Katherine Cramer Walsh, and two anonymous reviewers. I should thank the Robert Wood Johnson (RWJ) Foundation for funding the project while I was a Scholar in Health Policy at Harvard University. Theda Skocpol and Jennifer Hochschild were early champions of the project while I was an RWJ Scholar, and both provided critical insight on the research design and early drafts of the book. I should also thank my colleagues in the RWJ program—Sharon Bzostek, Hilary Levey Friedman, and Matthew Levy—who helped me wrestle with many of the conceptual and design issues that accompany the start of any major research project. Kathy Swartz provided crucial support for the project from start to finish.

There were many other people who also helped make the project a reality. I benefited from working with an excellent team of research assistants from Harvard and Wellesley including Ava Bramson, Devin Elliott, Jennifer Gu, Grace Park, Laurel Cadawalder Stolte, and Cait Toole. Barbara at New England Transcript was instrumental in transcribing the hours and hours of interviews with professionalism and care. Jason English helped me design figures for the book and helped me sharpen my thinking along the way. Kathryn Sargent Ciffolillo edited several versions of the book, making it better each time. I try to take every opportunity I can to thank Gretchen Brion-Meisels and Eliza Johnston for all that they do; in this case, I thank them for letting me use their parking pass on the countless days I holed myself up in the Diesel Café to work on the book without distraction. Finally, I can hardly imagine an editor better than Angela Chnapko at Oxford University Press.

Last but hardly least, I should thank my family. Hunter not only provided excellent feedback on a draft of the entire book, he also kept our household running while I traveled all over the country collecting data, and cheerfully picked up slack while I was preoccupied with writing. I know I have racked up considerable marital debt with this project; I look forward to paying it off. Even in his absence, Kaeson has been an integral part of this project. I started collecting data one month before we lost him and grieved him as the project went on. Through all of this, and throughout the project, Kaya has brought (and continues to bring) me endless joy just by being herself. By birth order and personality, Jaemin is the rainbow at the end of the storm. As I look into the future, Kaya and Jaemin are at the center of my hopes for the future of American democracy and our civic life. Kaeson is the anchor that reminds me why it matters.

H.H.

How Organizations Develop Activists

1

Introduction

One chilly morning in November 2010, I met "Paul" in a crowded coffee shop to interview him about his work as an environmental activist.[1] As we were waiting in line for our drinks, Paul warned me that he may not have much to say. "I know you're studying how to get people to do stuff," Paul said. "I wish I knew," he sighed. "We struggle with it every day."

This book begins with a simple question: why are some civic associations better than others at "getting"—and keeping—people involved in activism? By signing petitions, donating money, attending meetings, making phone calls, and joining with others, activists power American democracy. Yet, the challenge of "get[ting] people to do stuff" (or, as some might say, cultivating people's capacity for activism) is felt everywhere. From MoveOn.org to the National Rifle Association, Organizing for America to the Tea Party, from Health Care for America Now to the Sierra Club to local Parent-Teacher Organizations, membership-based civic associations constantly seek to engage people in civic and political action. What makes some more effective than others?

---

1. Throughout the book, the names of both individuals and organizations are disguised to maintain their anonymity. Interviewees from People for the Environment are given names that start with "P" while interviewees from the National Association of Doctors are given names that start with a "D." I discuss this commitment to anonymity further in the appendix, which is dedicated to discussing the methodological approaches used in this study.

To answer this question, I spent two years comparing organizations with strong records of activism to those with weaker records. I observed their behavior and ran some field experiments with them. In doing so, I tried to get into the guts of the organizations, to understand what makes some better able to generate and sustain activism than others. Is it just about a charismatic leader, the communities where they work, or the people they recruit? Or maybe it is their messaging or their ability to target recruits. Or maybe it is none of these things at all and is just plain luck.

All of these factors matter. But I found, in the end, that what really differentiates the highly active associations is the way they transform their members' motivations and capacities for involvement. Just as Alexis de Tocqueville predicted 200 years ago, the associations with the most breadth and depth of activism act as "great free schools of democracy." By blending contemporary online and offline tools, these associations build breadth and depth of activism by developing citizens as democratic leaders and engaging people in collective action. In doing so, these associations help lay the foundation for a healthy democracy.[2]

What surprised me was how much these highly active associations struggled to maintain a focus on the transformational work of building democratic citizens. Cultivating, and transforming, people's motivations and capacities for activism—"get[ting] people to do stuff" more often and with more depth—is not easy. It takes precious time and resources to develop relationships with members, cultivate their motivations, and teach them the skills of democratic citizenship. Civic associations are most likely to do this work when it helps them build power. As Theda Skocpol writes, "Democratic [organizing] becomes the norm when would-be leaders can achieve power and influence only by drawing others into movements, associations, and political battles. Elites must have incentives to organize others."[3]

---

2. Many scholars have examined the importance of civic associations in laying the foundation for a healthy democracy. See Fung 2003 for a summary of that research, and, especially, Skocpol 2003; Putnam 2001.

3. Skocpol 2003, 177.

Sometimes, contemporary political circumstances can create incentives for associations to abandon the long, patient work of leadership development. In the current environment, it can be tempting to short-circuit the process of developing activists by finding someone else who is already motivated and has the skills necessary for action. With the advent of new online technologies, big data, and analytics, finding these people—and getting to scale—is easier than ever before. Whereas getting a thousand signatures on a petition used to take weeks of pounding the pavement, now a well-crafted email to a targeted list can generate it in a matter of hours. Dramatic stories have been written about "viral engagements" such as Occupy Wall Street, the occupation of Tahrir Square in Egypt, the Susan G. Komen Foundation's decision to stop funding Planned Parenthood, and the shooting of Trayvon Martin in Sanford, Florida.[4] It seems like it is easier than ever to get people engaged in the twenty-first century, and the political process seems more open to citizen input. People power, perhaps, is on the rise.

Yet, many of the activists and associations I talked with have a vague unease that all this activity is not adding up to something bigger. To these observers, American democracy seems broken. People "do stuff" but problems persist. Widening gaps along income, social class, political ideology, race, religion, and other dimensions fragment our society.[5] Approval ratings of government plummet as political institutions fail to address the everyday problems people face.[6] Associations can get more people to engage in certain kinds of activism more easily than before, but many feel like they still lack the power they need to address fundamental problems of today's society. These activists and associations persistently questioned themselves: what can we do to develop the quantity and quality of activism we need to win the victories we want?

---

4. Fung and Shkabatur 2012.

5. See, for instance, Schlozman, Verba, and Brady 2012 for a discussion of rising inequalities and Brady and Nivola 2007 for a discussion of increasing polarization.

6. See Hibbing and Theiss-Morse 2001 and Hetherington 2005 for a discussion of declining trust over time.

That is why I wrote this book. Getting people involved in collective action is just one part of what civic associations do to build power—but it is fundamental. Models for how to engage people in activism, however, are not necessarily transparent in today's complex political environment. Providing these models is fundamental to helping these associations build the power they want and also to supporting our democracy. This book, thus, shows how organizations that combined transformational organizing with transactional mobilizing were able to achieve higher levels of activism over time.

Sometimes called "engagement organizing," "distributed organizing," or, in certain contexts, "integrated voter engagement," this blend of mobilizing and organizing helps civic associations build quality and quantity—or depth and breadth—of activism. To build power, civic associations need lots of people to take action and also a cadre of leaders to develop and execute that activity. They need individuals who take action but also a community that learns together how to translate that action into power. This is not a simple story about the power of offline versus online organizing. Instead, it is a story about how associations can blend both online and offline strategies to build their activist base. Associations face a constant tension between investing in membership and investing in members. Investing in membership helps build breadth, but investing in members helps build depth. I argue that associations do not have to choose between investing in members and investing in membership. They can do both. By investing in their members, they build the capacity they need to build their membership. This book describes how.

STUDY DESIGN

Figuring out what distinguishes associations that are good at generating and sustaining activism is no easy task. So many factors affect an association's ability to get people involved. Luckily, many scholars have come before me—because civic associations have long played an important role in American public life. According to the Washington Representatives Study, individual-based associations constitute 11.9 percent of the 12,000 organizations listed in the *Washington Representatives* directory.[7] These associations differentiate themselves from other types of organizations because they (a) make claims in the public arena, (b) depend on the voluntary actions of individual members, and (c) govern themselves through elected members.[8] Commonly referred to as citizen groups, these associations are often disproportionately prominent actors in political debates.[9] Part of what all of these associations do to build power is engage activists. Given the importance of this activism in the political process, lots of people have studied it. From studies of political participation, interest groups, social movements, and civic engagement, we already know a lot about what factors influence activism.[10]

We know, for instance, that the kinds of people associations attract (individual characteristics) and where the associations work (community characteristics) matter. To participate, a person must have the resources to do so (free time, civic skills, knowledge, and such) and they must want to participate.[11] Location also matters.[12] Civic associations located in areas

7. Schlozman, Verba, and Brady 2012.

8. See Knoke 1986; Andrews and Edwards 2004 for a discussion of the unique features of civic associations. Their reliance on voluntary action by members means that leaders must find ways to generate commitment instead of compliance, thus differentiating themselves from organizations that rely on paid employees and have more centralized bureaucracies (Kanter 1972).

9. According to the findings of Baumgartner et al. 2009, these civic associations are "the most frequently cited type of major participant in these policy debates" (9) and "may spend less on lobbying and lobby on fewer issues than business organizations, but when they do lobby, they are more likely to be considered an important actor in the policy dispute" (11, see also figure 1.1 on p. 13).

10. See, for instance, Klandermans and Oegema 1987; Rosenstone and Hansen 1993; Verba, Schlozman, and Brady 1995; Teske 1997b; Baumgartner and Leech 1998; Wilson and Musick 1999; Gerber and Green 2000; Polletta and Jasper 2001; Green and Gerber 2004, 2008; Schussman and Soule 2005; Beyerlein and Hipp 2006; Nickerson 2006; Arceneaux 2007; Klandermans 2007; Gerber, Green, and Larimer 2008; Musick and Wilson 2008; Munson 2009; Andrews et al. 2010; Dorius and McCarthy 2011; Eliasoph 2011; Garcia-Bedolla and Michelson 2012; Bimber, Flanagin, and Stohl 2012; Corrigall-Brown 2012; Karpf 2012; Kreiss 2012; Rogers, Gerber, and Fox 2012; Baggetta, Han, and Andrews 2013; and others.

11. Verba, Schlozman, and Brady 1995; Schlozman 2003.

12. Wandersman et al. 1987; Sampson, Morenoff, and Gannon-Rowley 2002; Zeldin and Topitzes 2002.

like San Francisco with an active, ideologically charged community can be better off than associations working in other areas.[13] Finally, the issue context can make a difference. Political opportunities can open up, for example, when issues become the subject of national attention through a major focusing event like Hurricane Katrina or a school shooting.

My study focuses on organizational factors—what an association can do to cultivate activism. A growing body of research reconceptualizes the choice to get involved in politics not as an individualized choice, but as one embedded in the complex social interactions people have.[14] Thinking about the choice this way raises the question about organizational factors: how can associations create the conditions that make it more likely people will take action? Many scholars have studied the different ways associations can frame their message, create incentives for people to participate, build targeted lists, and use other tactics for generating activism.[15] But we still lack a textured sense of how all of these tactics, when put together into a broader strategy for engagement, succeeds (or fails) in cultivating activism.

To examine this, I set up a two-phase study that tried to isolate the effect of organizational factors by combining observational and experimental data. The first phase consists of two-year, comparative case studies. In these case studies, I identified matched pairs of civic associations that were working on similar issues in similar communities and recruiting similar kinds of people—but differed in the levels of activism they inspired. If two associations are working on the same issue in the same kind of community and drawing the same kind of people, why is one more effective than the other at engaging people in action? I drew on surveys, interviews, and ethnographic observations to investigate this

---

13. Putnam 1995, 2000.

14. Garcia-Bedolla and Michelson 2012; Rogers, Gerber, and Fox 2012.

15. On framing, see Snow and Benford 1988; Snow 2007. On incentives for participation, see Wilson 1973; Miller 2005. On targeting, see Issenberg 2012; Kreiss 2012. For more on the way organizational contexts can affect participation, see summaries in Polletta and Jasper 2001, Snow, Soule, and Kriesi 2007, and Orum and Dale 2009.

question. Then, from this first phase, I identified key differences in what the high- and low-engagement local organizations did.[16]

I drew all of my matched pairs from two national associations that I am calling People for the Environment and the National Association of Doctors.[17] People for the Environment tries to get citizens engaged around environmental issues, and the National Association of Doctors seeks to get doctors and medical students involved in advocating for health reform. Both associations typify many of the characteristics common to modern civic associations. They have clear advocacy goals they are trying to achieve, they build power by engaging volunteers in activity, they govern themselves through elected leadership, and they operate at the national, state, and local levels. In addition, their local chapters operate relatively autonomously, such that we can examine variation in the local chapters to understand why some chapters are better than others at engaging people in activity, even though they operate within a common national framework. Each matched pair in my study consisted of local chapters working within the same national association. In total, I observed six pairs of local chapters in two national associations (twelve chapters total, six in each association).

The second phase of the project, the field experiments, built on hypotheses generated in the first phase to test their effectiveness in the context of online mobilization. Ultimately, to uncover causal relationships between actions an association takes and individual involvement, we need to test the effectiveness of different organizational interventions. These experiments examined how organizational actions affected the individual choice to take action.

Many more details on the research design are needed to fully understand the process I used to develop the arguments offered here. Together, chapter 2 and the appendix present those details—on everything from

16. As discussed in more detail in chapter 2, I define "high-engagement" organizations as those that historically have high rates of activism, while "low-engagement" organizations are those that historically have low rates of activism.

17. In undertaking the study with these associations, I agreed to preserve their anonymity. The choice to do so is discussed further in the appendix. In addition, I describe both associations more fully there.

the research design, to the two national associations that were the subject of study, to the implications of studying associations working on health and environmental issues, to the way I define activism, and the way I incorporate previous research. Here, let us get on to what I found.

MODELS OF ENGAGEMENT: LONE WOLVES, MOBILIZERS, AND ORGANIZERS

So what distinguished the high-engagement chapters who had strong historical records of engaging activists? The key distinction is that the high-engagement chapters combine some form of transformational *organizing* with transactional *mobilizing*. Organizers invest in developing the capacities of people to engage with others in activism and become leaders. Mobilizers focus on maximizing the number of people involved without developing their capacity for civic action. The high-engagement chapters did both. Low-engagement chapters either acted as *lone wolves* or focused solely on mobilizing. People often confuse mobilizing with organizing, but as this book will argue, they are quite different. When mobilizing, civic associations do not try to cultivate the civic skills, motivations, or capacities of the people they are mobilizing. Instead, they focus on maximizing numbers by activating people who already have some latent interest. Organizers, in contrast, try to transform the capacity of their members to be activists and leaders. The chapters with the highest levels of engagement in the study did both.

Associations, just like people, act with implicit theories of change in mind. A theory of change is a set of assumptions about what kinds of actions will produce desired outcomes. Some associations believe, for instance, that the best way to get people involved is to make it as easy as possible. Others believe that it is more important to give volunteers real responsibility, however complicated it may be. These, and other beliefs, come together to form a theory of how the association will achieve its goals.

In my research, the association leaders I spoke with identified three different theories of change, which translated into three different models of engagement: lone wolves, mobilizers, and organizers (the terms are taken from our interviews). Each model of engagement, described in table 1-1,

Table 1-1 COMPARISON OF LONE WOLF, MOBILIZING, AND ORGANIZING MODELS

	LONE WOLVES	Low-Engagement Sites Combined These Strategies / High-Engagement Sites Combined These Strategies — MOBILIZERS	ORGANIZERS
Strategy for building power	Build power through information	Build power by building membership; take people where they are	Build power by building leadership; transform motivations and capacities of members to take on more leadership
Strategy for building membership	N/A	Build membership by getting as many people as possible to take actions; build a bigger, more targeted prospect list	Build membership by developing leaders who can engage others; constantly develop leadership among new prospects
Implications for advocacy	Choose advocacy strategies that can be done without many people (i.e. writing comments, research)	Choose advocacy strategies that require quick engagement by lots of people (i.e. petitions); focus on reacting to timely events that engage people	Choose advocacy strategies that build people's engagement over time; focus on campaigns that sequence actions people can take
Implications for structure	Centralize responsibility in the hands of staff or a few key volunteers	Centralize responsibility in the hands of staff or a few key volunteers	Distribute responsibility out to a large network of volunteers
Implications for types of asks made to volunteers	N/A	Focus on discrete requests that often allow people to act quickly and alone	Focus on interdependent asks that are often more time-intensive, force people to work with others, and give them some strategic autonomy
Implications for communications with volunteers	Provide information and updates to interested people	Focus on reaching out to as many people as possible by developing attractive "pitches" that will draw in the most people and new networks	Focus on reaching out to people by building relationships and community with them
Implications for support	Minimal resources needed for training and reflection	Minimal resources needed for training and reflection	Need extensive resources for training, coaching, and reflection

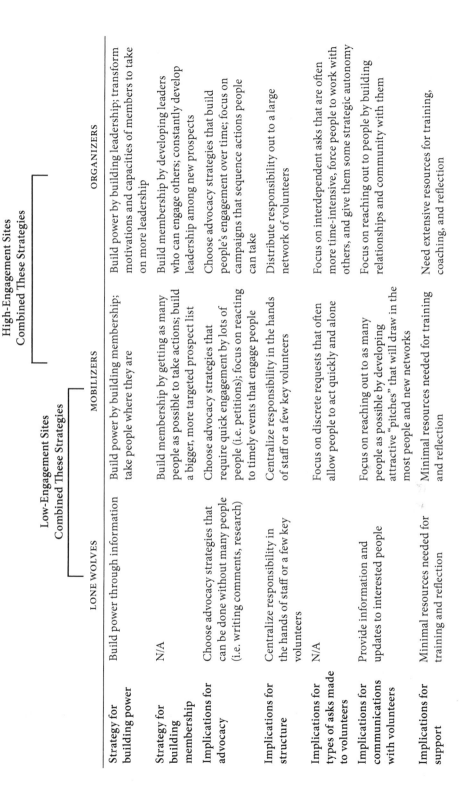

begins with a basic assumption about how to build power. This assumption drives subsequent choices listed in the table. Lone wolves choose to build power by leveraging information—through legal briefs, public comments, and other forms of research advocacy. Mobilizers and organizers, by contrast, choose to build power through people. Organizers distinguish themselves from mobilizers, however, because they try to transform the motivations and capacities of their members to cultivate greater activism. As Joy Cushman, the Campaign Director for PICO (a national network of faith-based community organizations) put it, "The organizer thus makes two [strategic] choices: 1) to engage others, and 2) to invest in their development. The mobilizer only makes the first choice. And the lone wolf makes neither."[18]

Lone Wolves

Peggy, for instance, is a long-time volunteer with People for the Environment and belongs to a chapter that is full of lone wolves. She initially got involved with People for the Environment because she was concerned about degradation of her local forest. When she first joined, she found that most of the other volunteers worked alone. So Peggy did the same thing. Over the years, she has developed an enormous body of knowledge about both the science of forest preservation and how the decision-making bodies relevant to protecting her local forest work—how and when they take public comment, what kinds of comments are most effective, how to participate effectively in the comment process, and so on. She devotes an enormous amount of time to this work, keeping abreast of policy developments, writing comments, attending hearings, and learning about the science and available policy alternatives. She is what other local leaders in People for the Environment call a "star volunteer," so her local chapter has given her responsibility for all forest protection work in their area. When asked what she has done to recruit volunteers to People

18. Personal communication, August 11, 2013.

for the Environment, however, she replied, "I'm so busy, I'm not doing anything and never have."

Lone wolves like Peggy do not put effort into engaging others. They choose advocacy strategies that do not require them to engage others and focus instead on building power by becoming an accurate source of information and expertise for decision-makers.[19] As exemplified by Peggy, they often do this because they do not have the resources to engage large numbers of people in their work, or they do not think it is important. Because they are part of membership-based associations, they still have to keep others updated, but they do so by providing others with information and updates about their work.

Mobilizers

Mobilizers build power by focusing on transactional outcomes like building the association's membership. They try to get as many people involved as possible, but they do not try to transform or cultivate volunteers' capacities for further activism. Instead, they take people where they are. Some people may act only once, and some may become involved over the long term. Some people may want to devote only a discrete amount of time to the association, while others may want to take responsibility for outcomes or become leaders. Mobilizers let people self-select the level of activism they want. To get enough people to accomplish their goals, mobilizers try to build the biggest, most targeted list possible, to maximize the chances they will find people poised for action.

David, for example, is a volunteer leader within the National Association of Doctors. He works with an informal group of about five doctors that initiates and carries out any strategic undertaking for the National Association of Doctors in its community. David and his team spent considerable time building their online presence through email, blogging, and social media. This online work has helped them amass

19. Hansen 1991; Smith 1995.

a rather long list of doctors who may be interested in the events and activities of the National Association of Doctors. In addition, they have developed partnerships with other progressive organizations such as the local Democratic Party, MoveOn, some unions, and other organizations. Putting those lists together with their own, they can reach a relatively wide audience to publicize upcoming events and activities for the National Association of Doctors. Once people are on the list, they send them information and a menu of opportunities for participation, and people self-select into actions they want to take.

Depending on the activity, David may get very robust or very low rates of participation. The more attractive his asks can be—such as if they are responsive to timely or controversial events in the news—the more likely he is to engage more people. In one instance, he wanted people to sign a petition and was able to generate hundreds of signatures online. In another instance, he tried to get doctors to attend an event he had organized with a speaker, and only two people showed up. When asked what works to engage people in action, he said, "Well, I keep pestering them. I send many emails and keep pestering basically." When asked how he followed up with the two people who showed up, David said, "Well, I didn't really talk to them, so I'm not sure who they are."

Because of the sheer number of events and activities they plan, David and his team engage a number of people in activity over time, but all of the responsibility for this work sits on their shoulders. When they cannot generate enough response to a request for action, they try to cast a bigger net. They try to search for and identify people who are poised for action. The bigger and more targeted their prospect pool, and the more responsive their asks can be to events in the news, the more likely they are to find larger numbers of people poised to respond to their requests for action.

Organizers

Phil's chapter in People for the Environment, by contrast, is full of organizers. When Phil first became a volunteer leader within People for the

Environment, he was given responsibility for organizing a certain geographic area in his state. Almost immediately, Phil realized that the area was too large for him to organize on his own. Other leaders within his state encouraged him to recruit other volunteers to help him organize his area and gave him some names of people to contact. Phil divided his area up into three sections and kept talking to people in those areas until he found three people who were willing to take responsibility for organizing each one. Then, he trained them in how to do their work, mimicking the training he had received when he first joined. Two of those leaders have recruited their own teams of people to help them, while one works alone. Now, Phil continues to meet with each of these three leaders on a weekly basis to check in about their work and to coach them in meeting their weekly goals. In describing this work, Phil says,

> [The three leaders and I had] talked about running this regional conference together.... For about a month [after we had the idea], I would have weekly calls with these three individuals around putting together the structure of how volunteers would run this conference—because we didn't have any funding.... It was their vision and their genius, and I was just kind of along for the ride with them, to help them create this structure and then recruit people. So they were the steering committee, and they recruited like eight of their friends, who they thought would each do a great job for their subcommittees. Those eight people joined the steering committee. And then the subcommittees, the chairs were responsible for recruiting for their committees. [There was a subcommittee on] conference content, fundraising, action, media, I can't remember the others, you know. Pretty soon, we had an active group of about 100 people working on developing this conference.

Phil and his team distribute responsibility for getting people involved across a number of leaders. His distributed leadership strategy depends on developing a subset of people as civic leaders and engaging them in collective action. Those leaders are invested with real responsibility, and Phil supports them in that work. Because he expects them to achieve certain outcomes, he also provides training and coaching to help them develop the skills and capacities they need to reach their goals. Engaging others in activism, then, depends not only on Phil, but on the network of leaders that he supports. Phil builds power by investing in the leadership skills of his activists and creating greater collective capacity by increasing the numbers of people responsible for engaging others in action. When Phil cultivates more leaders, Phil's chapter gains greater capacity to build power by engaging others in deeper ways.

COMPARING MOBILIZING AND ORGANIZING

Many scholars and practitioners confuse mobilizing and organizing. Lone wolf strategies are the most distinct because they do not focus on building power through people. The confusion between mobilizing and organizing arises, in part, because mobilizing and organizing are not mutually exclusive strategies. The local chapters with the highest rates of activism in this study did both. Not only are these local chapters able to mobilize large groups of people to take quick action, they also cultivate a group of people to become leaders. Nonetheless, distinguishing between these models of engagement is important for understanding how high-engagement sites attain their levels of engagement.

A core distinction of organizing is that it has the potential to be transformational in a way that other strategies do not. As Tocqueville argued in his observations of civic life in America in the 1830s, organizers bring individuals together in a way that creates a collective capacity not present when individuals act alone. Organizers do not simply aggregate individuals but also create new relationships between them that generate new commitments and resources.[20] Mark Warren described this phenomenon in his analysis of the Industrial Areas Foundation (IAF), a nationwide interfaith network of community organizers. "Those leaders who become and remain primary leaders in the organization ... speak of their participation in the IAF and its leadership development process as a transformative experience. They stay involved because they develop a 'self-interest' in personal growth and their newly won power."[21] Becoming a leader is a

20. Ganz 2009, 2010.

21. Warren 2001, 217.

transformative experience for activists within IAF, who reported developing a sense of personal agency that they previously lacked. Their work through IAF taught them that they could make a difference. By helping individuals discover and cultivate this sense of agency, the IAF organized them, pushing them in directions they might not have gone on their own.

Mobilizers, in contrast, do not seek to transform people's interests as they recruit them for action. They are focused instead on building their membership base—with more people on their list, they have a higher probability that more people can be activated for any given action. At any given time, some people are not ready to get involved while others are poised for action. People can be poised for action for a variety of reasons—perhaps they have a personal interest in health or environmental issues, or their interest was piqued by a news story they read, or they have a friend who is urging them to get involved, or they have some free time they are looking to fill.[22] Others may not be ready—because they are too busy, have other issues they care about more, or do not feel like their actions will make a difference. Mobilizers allow people to self-select the level of activism they desire.

Structurally, the work of mobilizing is usually centralized in the hands of a few leaders, while the work of organizing is distributed through a larger network of leaders. The primary goal of mobilizing is to generate transactional outcomes, such as large numbers of participants. Responsibility is often centralized in a group of people who seek to identity potential opportunities for participation and circulate it to an ever-widening group of potential activists. When there is a ready pool of people who can be easily activated because they have been primed by the media or by other events, mobilizing alone can sometimes achieve the transactional outcomes an association desires. Often, however, to reach its transactional goals at scale, an association needs a cadre of leaders who have the motivations, skills, and capacities to mobilize others. This cadre is developed through a distributed organizing structure. By focusing

---

22. See McAdam 1986 and Munson 2009 for a discussion about the importance of "biographical availability" in determining people's readiness for action.

on the transformational work of building long-term capacity, organizers build up the people-based "assets" of the association. The leaders that
organizers cultivate recruit future activists and leaders. The more responsibility is distributed to a wider network of organizers, the more capacity
the association has for mobilizing.

Because organizers seek to cultivate and transform people's interests,
they make different decisions from mobilizers about how to engage people
in action (as outlined in table 1-1). First, organizers make requests for
action that bring people into contact with each other and give them space
to exercise their strategic autonomy. Research shows that it is through
relationships and autonomus collective action that people's motivations
for action are likely to change, grow, and develop.[23] Working with other
people to strategize and take action is often challenging, however, because
it requires more time and coordination than working alone. Mobilizers
thus tend to focus on discrete, easy requests that allow people to act alone.
Because mobilizers are not worried about cultivating people's motivations, they are less concerned with bringing people into contact with each
other or giving them any strategic autonomy.

Second, and relatedly, organizers focus on building relationships and
community through interdependent (as opposed to individual) action.
The idea is that people's motivation for action and potential for learning
becomes centered on the relationships they have with other people in the
association.[24] James Q. Wilson argued that people have three different
types of motivations for getting involved in political organizations: purposive, solidary, and material. Purposive motivations have to do with
wanting to achieve particular policy goals. Solidary motivations are social and relational. Material motivations have to do with personal gain.
Mobilizers appeal mostly to purposive motivations, while organizers try
to appeal to all three, especially solidary ones. Mobilizers do not forge
strong enough relationships with the people they are trying to engage
to be able to use the relationships as a source of motivation. They focus

23. See Damasio 1994; Marcus, Neuman, and MacKuen 2000; Nussbaum 2001 for more on
the neurological basis of these findings.

24. Wilson 1973; Warren 2001.

instead on creating opportunities for participation that are as appealing as possible and then advertising (or marketing) those opportunities to as wide a list as possible.

Finally, because organizers want to develop people's ability to take responsibility, they focus on extensive training, coaching, and reflection, while mobilizers do not. Although both mobilizers and organizers may use outside strategies that depend on grassroots engagement for success, the ways in which they engage the grassroots are very different. Organizers make distinct choices about which activists they want to nurture as leaders, how to structure and develop relationships with activists and between them, how to cultivate the motivation and interests of potential activists and leaders, how to equip them with the skills they need to become leaders, and how to bring people together to engage in collective action.

Mobilizing and organizing are mutually reinforcing approaches. Mobilizing helps develop a prospect pool or "leads list" that can be used to identify potential leaders. Organizing can enable the work of mobilizing by developing high-quality leaders capable of recruiting future activists. To meet the challenges of building power, civic associations need to go broad in their mobilizing and deep in their organizing. The high-engagement chapters in this study, thus, did both.

PUTTING ORGANIZING AND MOBILIZING IN HISTORICAL CONTEXT: ONLINE VERSUS OFFLINE ACTIVITY

It is tempting to differentiate mobilizing and organizing strategies based on whether they are online or offline techniques. Online techniques lend themselves easily to mobilizing because they make targeting and list-building much easier and more efficient than before. Associations can build much larger and more targeted prospect pools with online technology than with traditional organizing strategies. The work of building relationships, fostering community, and creating interdependent work, in contrast, seems to depend largely on offline interactions. Indeed, much of the previous research on the organizational roots of activism focused on the importance of face-to-face activity and the creation of strong collective identities.[25] In fact, a robust debate has emerged about whether or not online tools can be effective vehicles for collective action. Critics of the new forms of political activity have argued that their focus on quick and easy tasks amounts to nothing more than mere "clicktivism," or worse yet, "slacktivism," replacing meaningful political action with shallow tasks.[26] As Malcolm Gladwell famously wrote in his critique of online activism, "the revolution will not be Tweeted."[27]

Simply equating mobilizing with online techniques and organizing with offline techniques would be a mistake, however. I argue that the important distinction between mobilizing and organizing is not whether the tools used are online or not. Both online and offline tools can be used effectively to mobilize and organize. Likewise, online and offline tools can be used ineffectively to mobilize and organize. As Bimber, Flanigan, and Stohl argue, debating whether specific technologies are able to do the kind of capacity building required for organizing is not useful because the technologies are changing so quickly.[28] While video-conferencing tools that were readily available to civic associations a few years ago were not able to foster the online collaboration needed in some forms of organizing, now they are much improved, much more accessible, and are only likely to get better. The question is not whether online or offline tools are better for organizing, but instead how changing technologies affect the landscape in which modern civic associations do their work.

Patterns of collective action have shifted throughout American history as the social, political, technological, and historical context has shifted. Democracy in America has never been a spectator sport. From the nation's founding, people have been joining together to make their voices heard in the political process. As Theda Skocpol ably documents, from

25. For summaries, see Polletta and Jasper 2001; Snow, Soule, and Kriesi 2007; Snow and Soule 2010.

26. e.g. Morozov 2009.

27. Gladwell 2010.

28. Bimber, Flanagin, and Stohl 2012.

the mid-nineteenth to the mid-twentieth century, much of this activity was organized through large, federated civic associations that spanned social classes. In these associations, "organizers [organized] organizers."[29] These organizers were "civicly ambitious men and women with national vision and power aspirations" who built national associations anchored in vibrant local chapters that worked together to "support [expansive] public social programs."[30]

This pattern of association activism changed, however, in the 1960s and 1970s with the advent of direct mail, the professionalization of movement organizations in the United States, and the fragmentation of associations based on social cleavages like race and gender. The advent of mass media—through television, direct mail, and such—in political communications allowed civic associations, for the first time, to communicate with members on a large scale. This change reduced incentives for organizing. As Skocpol writes, "[I]f mass adherents [can be] recruited through the mail, why hold meetings?"[31] More and more members of civic associations became "checkbook members," contributing a modest amount each year to maintain their membership but otherwise not participating in the organization in any way.[32] Associations that focused exclusively on mobilizing began to emerge.

The online revolution in the early 2000s has led to even more changes. Information now flows instantaneously, allowing associations to activate participation much more quickly than in the past. Associations that once relied on phone calls and monthly newsletters mailed to their members can now communicate instantaneously and interactively with members and supporters through a number of different mediums. Some scholars argue that the very structure of participation has changed, because individuals with computers no longer have to rely on large associations to organize their collective action, which has altered the way people think

29. Skocpol 2003, 89.

30. Skocpol 2003, 73.

31. Skocpol 2003, 210.

32. Berry 1999; Schier 2000; Skocpol 2003.

about membership in civic associations.[33] Associations now structure work and action around constantly shifting events and activities instead of long-standing associational rituals and programs.[34] Copious amounts of new data have become available to associations, allowing them to get immediate feedback on their outreach strategies and target their work far more effectively than before.[35] With all of these changes, participation has taken new forms. Many civic associations, like MoveOn.org, for example, rely primarily on Internet technologies, which has forced older civic associations, like the League of Women Voters, to adapt.

Just as the advent of mass media in the 1960s changed the context for political activism, so did the evolution of mass online communication. As the landscape of collective action changes with new technologies, the incentives for civic associations to engage in organizing change also. Online tools make the work of mobilizing much cheaper than before and allow associations to create bigger and more targeted prospect pools. This may enable some associations to reach their transactional goals for the number of people they want to engage in action without ever doing any organizing. In other words, with the ability to reach a bigger prospect pool that is more likely to take action because it is better targeted, associations may be able to get the number of signatures they need on a petition or the number of people they want at an event without having to invest in pushing people up the activist ladder. Thus, many associations first taking advantage of mass online communication have focused on mobilizing.

Whether this is a durable long-term strategy for the association still remains to be seen. Some, like Zeynep Tufecki, argue that focusing solely on digital mobilizing might "paradoxically…[engender] hindrances to movement impacts…related to policy and electoral spheres."[36] These hindrances emerge, Tufecki argues, because the ability of digital tools to reduce the costs of coordination and communication also means

33. Bennett 2012; Bimber, Flanagin, and Stohl 2012; Karpf 2012; Mele 2013.

34. Karpf 2012.

35. Issenberg 2012; Kreiss 2012.

36. Tufecki 2014.

that associations relying on them are never forced to create leadership structures that later enable them to exercise power. They achieve their transactional goals, in other words, without ever engaging in the transformational work of organizing. Associations like MoveOn, which were at the vanguard of using online tools to mobilize people for action,[37] have begun to realize the limits of transaction without transformation. Mobilizing by itself can work if an association does not need to engage large numbers of people very consistently or does not need them to engage in very intensive activism, or if it has other sources of power other than people power. In that case, mobilizing may be a cheap and effective strategy to reach transactional engagement outcomes. For associations that do not have large prospect pools, that need people to engage in acts that require more time or risk, or that depend consistently on people to maintain power, mobilizing strategies alone may be of limited efficacy.

Given some of the limitations of mobilizing alone, a newer model of engagement, sometimes called "engagement organizing" or "distributed organizing," that blends mobilizing and organizing began to emerge near the end of the first decade of the twenty-first century. In 2006–2007, MoveOn stopped relying exclusively on its online mobilizing model and shifted toward developing local offline "Leadership Councils" and other structures to enhance their organizing ability. Similarly, in 2007–2008, the campaign to elect Barack Obama president developed a model of blending online and offline organizing and mobilizing.[38] The shift in the strategies employed by MoveOn and the Obama campaign, as well as other developments, demonstrated the power that civic associations can create by blending online and offline mobilizing and organizing. Many of the most vibrant civic associations working online today, as a result, are exploring ways of organizing using online tools—they are working to create tools that can help enable the kinds of transformations that make organizing possible.

All of the models of engagement described in this book—transactional mobilizing, transformational organizing, and ways to blend the two approaches—emerged historically as associations responded to changing

37. Karpf 2012.

38. McKenna and Han 2014.

technologies, information economies, and political pressures. Each new information regime introduces uncertainty for associations about how to leverage new technologies and build power in the new terrain.[39] This whirlwind tour of changing historical patterns of mobilizing and organizing in American politics demonstrates the fundamental point that widespread organizing becomes more likely when civic associations need to organize to build power. Civic associations are most likely to engage in the hard work of organizing when they see it as a way for them to meet their goals. In the contemporary era, the affordances created by digital tools can sometimes enable associations to reach their transactional engagement goals with mobilizing alone—making it seem, in the contemporary environment, that the hard work of transformational organizing is not needed. For associations feeling the limits of transactional mobilizing, however, alternate models of engagement need to be clear. This book presents those alternate models.

This incentive structure linking models of engagement to association power, however, exists whether or not online tools for collective action are available. New technologies for communication and collaboration, new data, and new modes and structures of participation have not changed the core principles that differentiate transformational organizing from transactional mobilizing. Whether associations are using online or offline tools, if they want to develop the capacity of people to engage in further activism and become leaders, they have to create opportunities for transformation by developing interdependent, autonomous venues for participation, forging a sense of community, and training people in the online and offline skills they need to become leaders or deepen their activism. In both the online and offline context, in other words, the core lessons from this book remain true. While some debate whether the changes wrought by the new information age are "good" or "bad," or "effective" or "ineffective,"[40] I argue that the more important question is about how associations use these new tools to engage activists. The important distinction is not whether the tools

39. Bimber 2003.

40. Morozov 2009; Gladwell 2010.

are online or offline, but instead how the associations use various tools to build power. This book thus describes how civic associations cultivate political activists and develop civic leaders in the modern era.

CHAPTER OVERVIEW

The following chapters explore the ways in which civic associations act as mobilizers and organizers to cultivate activism and leadership. Chapter 2 sets the stage for the study by diving into more of the theory and method behind the study. I consider alternative possibilities that could explain the differences between high-engagement and low-engagement sites. Perhaps high-engagement sites engage more people because they are in more politically active communities, or because they attract people who are more interested in activism. To address these possibilities, chapter 2 describes the similarities within the pairs of high- and low-engagement chapters selected for study in the People for the Environment and the National Association of Doctors. I draw on individual- and community-level data to ask whether and how the individual traits of members and community characteristics differ across the high- and low-engagement chapters. While minor differences do exist, they are not sufficient to explain the statistically significant gaps in rates of activism observed across these local chapters. Yet, I show that the high-engagement chapters were consistently able to engage more people than the low-engagement chapters during the period of the study. Why? Given the similarities in the communities they worked in and the individuals who joined, what explains these differences?

The appendix contains a further description of the methodology used in this study and supplements the information in chapter 2. Details are provided in the appendix so that they do not interrupt the narrative flow for readers less inclined to wade through the methodological weeds. For interested readers, the appendix describes (a) the process used to select the two national associations included in the study; (b) more detail on the two associations, their place in the broader landscape of civic associations, their relationships to the local chapters, and their overall functioning;

(c) details on how the high- and low-engagement locals included in the comparative case study were selected; (d) descriptions of the community and structural characteristics of the locals included in the comparative case study; (e) demographic and political profiles of the new members joining these local chapters; (f) a detailed discussion of the literature behind the alternative hypotheses explaining differences between high- and low-engagement chapters; and (g) a description of my relationship to the associations in the study.

Chapter 3 continues the argument by examining the myriad factors that come together to influence the way association leaders interpret their strategic environment, make choices about whether to organize or mobilize, and the divergent structures of responsibilities that ensue. It describes how many of the high-engagement chapters that chose to organize did so as the result of some kind of exogenous challenge that pushed them to adopt an organizing approach. Some of the chapters, like Phil's, faced a resource constraint. They had to organize a larger geographic area than they were able to cover with paid staff or existing leaders, or they needed to engage more people than they were able to with existing staff and volunteer leaders. As a result, they began to organize to turn more activists into leaders, so that a larger group of people could share the burden of the work. Many of the high-engagement chapters in the study had similar historical, episodic reasons that forced them to invest a larger number of volunteer leaders with responsibility. Depending on the way they interpreted the challenges they faced and the choices they had before them, many opted to organize and to invest in developing the capacity of volunteers to become leaders. In addition, this chapter describes the way the choice to organize or mobilize has important structural implications. I describe the structural differences between the way a lone wolf model, a mobilizing model, and an organizing model distributes leadership responsibilities. Once sites develop the practice of organizing or mobilizing, however, it has a strategic "stickiness" (or path dependence) to it that makes it more likely they will continue to organize in the future. This chapter argues that the choices local chapters make about what kind of strategy to pursue depend on a complex set of factors including the challenges the chapter faces, the way it interprets and makes sense of those challenges, the individual biographies of the leaders involved, and the structures the chapter has in place.

This observed path dependence demonstrates the reciprocal relationship that exists between individuals and organizational contexts. Organizational cultures and narratives shape individuals within the chapter and the ways in which those individuals make meaning out of the world around them. At the same time, these individuals bring their own histories, experiences, and perceptions to the chapter, thus shaping the organizational context. When Phil first joined People for the Environment, he had not been trained as an organizer and did not know how it worked. Yet, he liked working with people, had worked with teams of people through student organizations in college, and was open to finding and learning different ways of doing things. When he took responsibility for an entire geographic area, he learned to organize from the example of other volunteer leaders within the chapter who had been organizing as a way of achieving their goals. His choice was influenced by the fact that other volunteer leaders he worked with had been organizing, that people who preceded him had worked as organizers, and that he was part of an informal social network of volunteer leaders in his state who all took an organizing approach. The way he learned to be a leader, in other words, was shaped by the organizational context, but he was the one who made choices about how to engage people in his geographic area.

Chapters 4 and 5 describe in greater depth the organizational practices that differentiate organizers and mobilizers. Chapter 4 delineates the distinctions between transactional mobilizing and transformational organizing more clearly, and the implications each approach has for how local chapters engage activists in advocacy work. Associations focused on transformational organizing are more likely to engage volunteers in work that brings them into contact with each other, gives them some strategic autonomy, and shows them how their work fits into a larger whole. Even in modern civic associations that use Internet technologies for mobilizing and organizing, time-tested techniques of relationship-building and investing in people's development form the core of successful organizing strategies. These relational commitments become an important source of motivation. The commitment to activism, then, is borne not only of commitment to the issue but also of commitment to other people. In addition, local leaders provide extensive feedback to activists and reflect intentionally with members so that they begin to understand their own actions in light of their own agency. I describe the differences in the ways high- and low-engagement chapters make requests of their members and support their activism. As they ask individuals to engage in activism and then support them in their work, high-engagement chapters build strong interpersonal relationships with the activists and invest in their skills and motivations as leaders. This focus on long-term relational work differentiates them from the low-engagement chapters.

Chapter 5 focuses on the question of how associations achieve scale even as they do transformational organizing. I describe strategies chapters use to mobilize their members to achieve transactional outcomes at scale. I show how chapters blending mobilizing and organizing used mobilizing strategies that had beneficial downstream effects for the association by laying the foundation for future organizing. For instance, in the process of building lists of potential activists, low-engagement chapters are more likely to use relatively passive marketing strategies that allow them to post information and wait for people to consume it. High-engagement chapters are more likely to target people more directly and encourage more interactive activity, using strategies that helped the chapter build leadership skills and motivations among leaders. The high-engagement chapters thus bring far more intentionality to their mobilizing, building the capabilities of leaders even as they mobilize to continually expand their capacity to mobilize at scale. I draw on observational data to describe different kinds of strategies and also the findings of three experimental studies testing the effect of different online strategies in recruiting activists. These experiments test some of the strategies used by high-engagement chapters to generate transactional outcomes while still creating beneficial downstream effects. These studies show that the extent to which the association seeks to develop activist identities makes a difference in whether people respond to the request for action. The organizational activities, in other words, matter.

Chapter 6 concludes the book. I begin by reviewing the findings from previous chapters and discuss the ways in which they are distinct from previous research and conventional wisdom on activism. Because data in the book come from research with two major civic associations, I also discuss the external validity of these findings, examining publicly available data on mobilizing practices of other associations to show important commonalities across them. I then discuss existing research on the sources of political activism and recast the literature in light of the new findings from the book. The chapter also discusses the implications of this research not only for scholarship but also for practice. What are the policy and practical implications of this work? I argue that the book develops key insights into ways to mobilize traditionally hard-to-mobilize populations. Many people report believing that civic and political involvement is important, but many fewer people get involved. Identifying association strategies that can catalyze individual motivations to engage in activism brings us one step closer to understanding how to close the gap between intention and action.

CONCLUSION

Democracy works when people exercise their right to have a voice in the political system—but democracy fails when people do not, or do not do it very thoroughly. By attending rallies; contacting elected officials and media; reaching out to neighbors, friends, and family; and otherwise expressing their views in the public arena, activists play an important role in American politics. They disproportionately see their views enacted in policy outcomes and are crucial for mobilizing others to participate. In a Tocquevillian sense, activists are the threads that hold the social and political fabric of America together. Many of these activists become involved through civic associations. Some 79 percent of activists report getting involved through a civic association.[41]

41. Verba, Schlozman, and Brady 1995, 62.

By bringing people together for collective activity, associations teach people the basic skills of democratic citizenship while advocating for their members' interests in the public arena. Civic associations have the potential to cultivate and nurture democratic participation to create new models for collective action. Through the ways in which they reach and engage people, these associations can become engines of activism that propel people to higher levels of involvement. This book examines the way in which modern associations do that by examining their engagement strategies from the perspective of both the association and the volunteer.

A strong body of research on civic and political participation already informs our understanding of activism. While building on this previous research, this book also differs from it in three important ways. First, most prior work is based on research with civic associations that pre-date the Internet revolution. Second, prior research focuses more on the act of joining or affiliating with an association than on the choice to engage in ongoing activity. Third, there is little research on civic leadership in particular. By examining how modern civic associations blend mobilizing and organizing to develop activists and leaders, I uncover the core principles that make it possible for civic associations to engage people in civic and political action, develop their democratic capacities, and build the foundation on which our democracy rests. People power the associations; this book describes how associations power people.

2

Setting up the Comparative Case Studies

At the core of this study is an important puzzle uncovered by the data I collected: even though the same kinds of people joined high- and low-engagement chapters, the high-engagement chapters were able to consistently engage more people in activism than the low-engagement chapters. In other words, the members were the same but the participatory outcomes were different. Figure 2-1 depicts these differences.

At the beginning of my study, I identified a group of individuals who had just joined the National Association of Doctors and People for the Environment. I surveyed them about a range of topics, including their personal backgrounds, their reasons for joining, and their previous activity in civic associations. Then, I compared the characteristics of people joining the chapters with historically low levels of engagement to those joining chapters with historically high levels of engagement. As discussed in more detail later in this chapter, and as shown in figure 2-1, the differences at the outset were minimal. When people first joined the National Association of Doctors and People for the Environment, those joining high-engagement organizations were no more likely to be active in civic associations than those joining low-engagement organizations (the differences between these groups were about 4 percentage points in both associations and were not statistically significant).

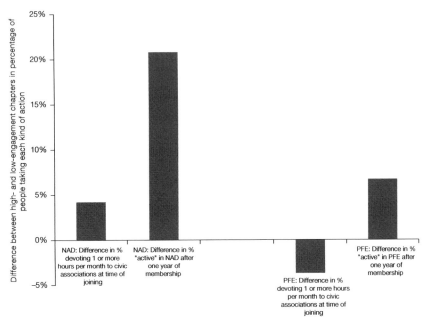

Figure 2-1. Differences between Levels of Engagement in High- and Low-Engagement Chapters at the Beginning of the Study and after One Year of Membership

I surveyed these same people one year after they had joined the National Association of Doctors and People for the Environment, however, and found that those in high-engagement chapters were much more likely to have taken action than those in low-engagement chapters. Both the National Association of Doctors and People for the Environment had their own definitions of who they counted as an "activist" within the organization. The National Association of Doctors counted anyone who had taken three or more actions online, or any action offline as an activist. People for the Environment counted anyone who had taken five or more actions online, or any action offline as an activist. As shown in figure 2-1, people in high-engagement chapters in the National Association of Doctors were over 20 percentage points more likely to have been activists, while the difference in People for the Environment was about 7 percentage points (both differences statistically significant at $p < 0.1$). These people had been very similar to each other—on a number of dimensions, as I show further in this chapter—when they first joined the National Association of Doctors and People for the Environment, but they diverged in their

patterns of activism after one year. What did the high-engagement organizations do differently?

Teasing out these differences—and similarities—between the low- and
high-engagement chapters in the study lays the foundation for my broader
argument. In the book, I argue that *how* civic associations engage their
members in activism affects the quantity and quality of activism they can
develop. But what if differences between the high- and low-engagement
chapters can be explained by factors other than the way they mobilize or
organize their members? What if the high-engagement chapters are not,
in fact, reliably engaging their members in activism? This chapter considers those potential objections to the argument.

I show that while some contextual and individual differences between
the local chapters exist, they are not enough to explain the differences
in patterns of engagement. I also dive more deeply into the previous research, simultaneously defining more precisely what I mean by activism
and what the implications of activism are for our democracy. Much research on the sources of political activism emphasize the individual characteristics, traits, and life circumstances that affect a person's willingness
to participate, or the broader contextual factors (such as characteristics of
the larger social movement) that push people to get involved. This book
examines a middle tier of factors—characteristics of the local chapters
and the effectiveness of different organizational strategies in motivating
political activism. This chapter lays the foundation for this argument by
defining what is known about activism first, and then examining the individual and contextual differences that characterize the distinct experiences of people in low-engagement and high-engagement chapters.

WHAT IS CIVIC AND POLITICAL ACTIVISM AND
LEADERSHIP?

Political activists play myriad roles in American politics. Activists sign
petitions, contact their elected officials, show up at hearings over regulatory issues, broadcast news through social media, attend rallies and
events designed to show their support (or disdain) for a particular cause,

write letters to the media, and join with other individuals to address community issues. Through what they say, what they do, and how they allocate precious resources (like time and money), activists express their preferences to government officials. Because the message is stronger when multiplied, activists often try to recruit others to join them in expressing the same message. By joining with others to make their voices heard and devoting time and resources to politics, activists lubricate our democracy, taking advantage of—and often creating—participatory opportunities.

For the purposes of this book, I focus on activism within civic associations. I define associational activism as intensive voluntary activity with a civic association that has the intent or effect of influencing decision-makers with power. Several noteworthy features of this definition emerge. The first three features are consistent with definitions of participation commonly used in scholarly studies.[1] First, I focus on *activity*, on taking some form of civic or political action, as opposed to merely paying attention to it (reading the paper, following current events), or having an opinion about it. Second, I focus on activity designed to influence seats of *power*, whether it be governmental, corporate, or other decision-makers who control resources. It is important to note that the actions individuals take may not be political, even if the civic association has a political agenda. Research has shown that associations often get people involved through non-political activity.[2] For instance, the Sierra Club, a national environmental association, engages people by inviting them to go on hikes. I include this kind of associational activity in my definition, however, because these civic associations often try to engage people in explicitly political activity after they get hooked through recreational hikes and other such actions. Third, I focus on activity that is *voluntary*. Activists are people whose activity is not obligatory in any way.

The fourth feature of this definition of activism—its characterization as "intensive" activity—is the most challenging to define. Participation

1. See, e.g., Verba, Schlozman, and Brady 1995.

2. e.g., Munson 2009; Baumgartner and Leech 1998; Walker 1991; see Murray 2012 for an application of this idea to the contemporary political environment.

is a continuum, with people who do not participate at all at one end and activists who devote their lives to political activity at the other end. Somewhere along that continuum, activity changes from being an isolated, incidental act to an "intensive" act that is integrated into a person's life and requires him or her to make choices to devote time and/ or other resources to political activity. This is not attending one meeting and never coming back, or responding to one email but never participating again. The book explores the roots of intensive political activism, the circumstances under which people make a sustained commitment to political activity. Intensive activism means that people regularly read the emails they are sent and respond actively; show up to the rallies, hearings, and meetings; and take time out of their daily lives to do work for the association.

Political activity can be "intensive" along several different dimensions, including the time commitment involved (such as attending weekly meetings of a civic association) and the effort it entails (such as the material resources needed, the risk involved in participation, and other costs incurred by the participant).[3] Some forms of participation are limited in time and effort, such as signing a petition once. Other forms of participation can be more demanding in terms of effort than of time, such as participating in a rally for one day. Still other forms of participation can be intensive in terms of time, such as reading through all the emails associations send and choosing which ones to respond to by taking action. Finally, some forms of participation are demanding in terms of both time and effort, such as voluntarily leading a local community group. In this book, I examine activism that is intensive along at least one dimension, time or effort.

Leadership is a subset of activism. I define leadership as Marshall Ganz has done, "accepting the responsibility to engage others in achieving purpose in times of uncertainty."[4] Civic associations often operate in conditions of uncertainty, in which leaders have to make strategic choices about allocating resources under highly contingent circumstances with

3. Klandermans 2007.

4. Ganz 2010.

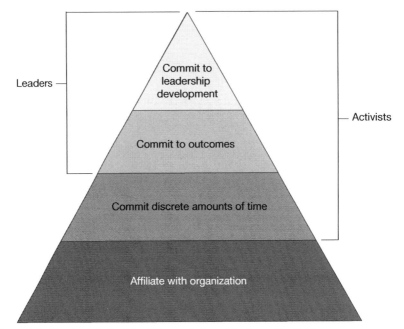

Figure 2-2. The Activist Ladder (Figure designed by Jason English)

unclear outcomes.[5] Leaders are those who take responsibility for engaging others in navigating this uncertainty, helping them achieve their goals in a way that is consistent with their values. Leadership, then, is a form of activism that is intensive in terms of both time and effort; it involves ongoing commitment to activity in a civic association. Leaders are distinct from activists because they take responsibility for outcomes, as opposed to merely showing up.

We can imagine an "activist ladder" within civic associations (see figure 2-2); anyone on or above the second rung is an "activist," while only those at the top two rungs of the ladder are "leaders."[6] On the bottom rung of the ladder are the many people who merely affiliate with the association, whether by paying dues to become a member, making a single financial contribution, or otherwise getting on the association's list of

5. Ganz 2009; Morris and Staggeborg 2007.

6. This activism ladder is frequently used within People for the Environment to refer to volunteers at different levels of activism. The differentiations they make between each level of activism are applicable to both civic associations in the study.

supporters. Activists move up to the second rung, in which they commit discrete amounts of time to the association. This might involve showing up for meetings, participating in a phone bank, signing an online petition, tweeting information through social media, or participating in another activity that does not require the volunteer to take on any responsibility. The third rung includes volunteers who take responsibility for some outcome, who commit whatever time it takes to achieve an outcome for which they are responsible. This might involve getting 50 people to show up to an event, getting 100 signatures on a petition, or even shepherding a piece of legislation through the legislature. Activists on this third rung have a sense of personal accountability for achieving the outcome and will put in whatever time and effort it takes to achieve it. Finally, on the fourth rung of the activist ladder are people who take responsibility not only for achieving outcomes but also for developing others as activists and leaders. They have a sense of personal accountability for ensuring the long-term health of the association by constantly developing a stable of volunteers, activists, and leaders who will continue to move up the activist leader.

To achieve their policy goals, civic associations often need people at all levels of the activist ladder. Mobilizers focus primarily on building the number of people at the bottom two rungs of the ladder. Organizers focus on building numbers and quality throughout, focusing particularly on building capacity at the top two rungs of the ladder. Organizers assume that developing high-quality leaders at the top will enable them to recruit more people on the bottom two rungs. High-engagement sites in the study did both mobilizing and organizing, thus building the number and quality of activists and leaders at all rungs of the ladder.

Much prior research focuses on people at the bottom two rungs of the activist ladder rather than on people who are higher up.[7] This might be because only a minority of the American population engages in any kind

---

7. Exceptions to this include a set of in-depth case studies of civic associations such as Barakso 2004; Rothenberg 1992; Warren 2001; and many others. As discussed elsewhere, many of these studies focus on older forms of collective action that have now changed with the advent of new technologies for collective action created by the Internet. This book focuses on modern-day civic associations, and both online and offline techniques.

of civic and political action. Estimating the precise percentage of people who count as "activists" is challenging because definitions vary. In their 1990 Citizen Participation Study, Verba, Schlozman, and Brady find that while 71 percent of people report voting, only 24 percent report making campaign contributions, and only 8 percent report having volunteered for a campaign.[8] As the activity becomes more demanding, the number of people who engage in that kind of activism drops sharply. Almost half of all respondents (48 percent) to the Citizen Participation Study reported affiliation with some political association, but less than one-third (29 percent) report having attended a meeting of a political association. Similar patterns emerge for other forms of political activity. Thirty-four percent of respondents report having initiated contact with a government official, while only 6 percent report having engaged in some form of protest activity. Seventeen percent report having engaged in informal community activity, while 14 percent report having attended a meeting of an official local board, and only 3 percent report having served on a local board or council. Depending on the point of comparison, these numbers can be interpreted as "small" or "large."[9] The fact remains, however, that only a minority of the American public engages in intensive political activity.

This study focuses on people engaged in activity at the top three rungs of the ladder. It does not examine the reasons some people affiliate with civic associations and others do not. Many researchers have examined the initial decision to become active, such as the choice to join an association.[10] Joining is the first rung of the activist ladder. With respect to the higher rungs of the ladder, debate continues about what conditions predict whether a person is going to engage in ongoing activism.[11] Although the factors that influence a person's decision to join an association are

8. Verba, Schlozman, and Brady 1995, 50–52.

9. For further discussion of the relative magnitude of these numbers, see chapter 3 in Verba, Schlozman, and Brady 1995.

10. e.g., Walker 1991; Olson 1965; Baumgartner and Leech 1998; Verba, Schlozman, and Brady 1995.

11. Beyerlein and Hipp 2006; Corrigall-Brown 2012; Klandermans and Oegema 1987; Schussman and Soule 2005; Wilson and Musick 1999; Eliasoph 2011; Musick and Wilson 2008.

likely related to the factors that influence the decision to persist in activism within the association, we cannot assume that they are the same. People often join civic associations for episodic reasons that are tied to accidents of biography (they are experiencing a life transition and need a social outlet, for example).[12] Once in the association, some of these people become very active and others do not. While part of the explanation is related to biographical availability, other factors—related to what the associations do to engage them and how they do it—may matter as well.

In addition, very little previous work looks specifically at civic leaders and the roots of their leadership.[13] Yet, many political associations face the challenge of moving people up the activist ladder on a daily basis. Civic associations not only need large numbers of people to call legislators or show up to rallies—but also depend on leaders who make the association run. These people pore over regulatory statements to interpret them for other volunteers and attend weekly meetings to deal with the administrative side of running the association. They plan events and reach out to others to get them to attend those events. They organize petition drives and phone banks to ask other volunteers to attend. For civic associations to function, they need a cadre of leaders to devote their time, but little research has been done on the strategies that are most effective in getting people involved at the leadership level. Leading a civic association is a very different task from signing an online petition or attending a house party. While these actions are all forms of political activism, they are differentiated in many ways, including the degree of uncertainty entailed, the need for strategic capacity, and the focus on interpersonal interactions.

This book probes organizational factors that affect a continuum of activism, from those who commit small and incidental amounts of time to those who become leaders. Why are some associations better than others at organizing people to move up the activist ladder?

12. Munson 2009.

13. Morris and Staggeborg 2007; Dorius and McCarthy 2011.

WHY STUDY ACTIVISM AND LEADERSHIP WITHIN
CIVIC ASSOCIATIONS?

During the 2009–10 debate over health care reform, the National Association of Doctors enjoyed considerable access to elected officials as both a pathway for their work and a recognition of the impact they had. A volunteer leader describes the role the National Association of Doctors played in swaying legislators from that state to vote for reform:

> I still don't know to this day how, but one day I got a call on my office phone out of the blue from [our] Congressman.... At the time he was a not very prominent [member], but he had heard about our group. He wanted to come up and meet with us, so we said "Sure." By the time he came to meet with us, the first vote had taken place and he voted against healthcare reform. That's not right. [At our meeting], eight doctors each presented a reason why healthcare reform was important... and then he shared with us his concerns.... All of this stuff goes on and he [starts calling] my cell phone number. I'm getting calls from the Congressman directly to me—almost like back door consultations, [asking] "What do you think about this, really?" I was so amazed that we were in the position to offer this sort of guidance and I had four or five calls with him. When the last week of the debate [in March 2010] came up, I really lobbied him and really poured it on.... After the vote, I actually spoke to [the Congressman], and he was cited as one of the five pivotal votes in the final hour by *Politico*.... So I asked him "Did we play a role in your vote?" He said, "Absolutely because I felt like you had my back. I felt like I had a group of doctors out there who would say this is a good thing from a medical point of view." So we really felt like we played a role in one of the pivotal votes.

Although activists constitute a relatively small part of the American population, they have an impact disproportionate to their numbers. Another prominent example of the power of activists to capture policy debate emerged during the campaign to pass health care reform in 2009 and 2010. Throughout the negotiations over the bill that ultimately became the Affordable Care Act, Tea Party activists played a large role in shaping the legislation. In their analysis of the debate over health care reform, Lawrence Jacobs and Theda Skocpol considered the question, "What did outside pressures accomplish?" They wrote, "Because they were mobilized and intensely focused potential voters for the GOP, Tea Partiers and other right-wing activists were a large part of the reason Republicans in Congress would not visibly engage or formally compromise as health reform bills progressed, driving the breakdown in visible bipartisanship."[14] Through their activism, Tea Party activists constrained Republicans' ability to compromise on key features of the bill, pushing the legislation in particular directions.

Other scholarly research also shows that activists help lobbying groups achieve power in the political process. In their expansive study of lobbying, Baumgartner et al. found that activist-based civic and political associations—citizen groups—are disproportionately represented as important actors in policy debates. The factor most related to these organized interests' "winning" in a policy debate is having access to elected officials. For citizen groups, generating this access—and thus, power—depends on their ability to mobilize members through the help of activists.[15] Even for advocacy groups that are not citizen-based, mobilizing citizens is a tactic commonly used to build power. Some 47.7 percent of advocacy groups mobilize mass membership as part of their advocacy tactics.[16] That is the most common tactic outside of inside lobbying of members of Congress (i.e., personal contact with members, etc.). As different lobbying interests seek to organize citizens for political activity, in other words, they depend on activists to help them nurture and build their power base. Understanding the ways in which interest groups mobilize citizens can provide insights into the ways these groups build power in the political system.

Activists also shape the participation of others. Since Rosenstone and Hansen's seminal study, scholars have recognized the importance of recruitment in generating participation.[17] More recently, experimental studies of participation have found that this recruitment is most effective

14. Jacobs and Skocpol 2010, 82.

15. Baumgartner et al. 2009, 156–157.

16. Baumgartner et al. 2009, table 8.1, 151.

17. Rosenstone and Hansen 1993.

when it is nested in an authentic person-to-person interaction. Initial studies found that door-to-door canvassing is generally more effective than phone calls or other forms of mobilization.[18] Subsequent studies found, however, that personalized phone messages delivered in a conversational manner may be as effective as in-person canvassing.[19] What really matters in making recruitment effective, in other words, is the dynamic human interaction between two people.[20] Activists can play an important role in making this happen, particularly in campaigns and organizations that rely on volunteers for on-the-ground organizing.

Beyond the important roles activists play in shaping policy outcomes and generating participation among others, activists have normative importance within a democracy (discussed further in Appendix). Civic associations help make American democracy work, Tocqueville argued, because they help ordinary individuals develop the skills and motivations they need to participate in civic and political action. By voluntarily engaging in causes with each other, activists learn to articulate their concerns, express their opinions, act with each other, and take actions to advance their own goals. They constantly develop, support, and exercise their own agency as democratic citizens and, in doing so, create an informal societal infrastructure that helps make democratic freedoms and equality possible.[21] Modern democratic theorists such as Carole Pateman and Benjamin Barber agree. Participation has inherent value in its ability to transform passive subjects into citizens. Barber argues that participation in public life takes potential abilities and turns them into action, helping people develop the capacities and motivations they need to advance.[22] Activism in public life matters because it makes democracy possible.

18. Gerber and Green 2000; Green and Gerber 2004.

19. Nickerson 2006; Arceneaux 2007.

20. Gerber and Green 2000; Green and Gerber 2004; Garcia-Bedolla and Michelson 2012.

21. Tocqueville [1835–40] 1969.

22. Orum and Dale 2009, 287–288.

Given their normative importance, as well as the disproportionate influence of those who do get involved, understanding more about who these activists are and how they become so involved is important to understanding American democracy. Understanding the sources of activism necessitates an examination of civic associations. Verba, Schlozman, and Brady find that 79 percent of respondents in their study of activists reported being involved at some minimal level with some association (including political and non-political associations), and 41 percent reported having four or more affiliations.[23] Likewise, 63.4 million people (26.8 percent) reported participating in public life through or for a civic association at least once between September 2008 and September 2009 in the Current Population Survey.[24] Through membership, making financial contributions, attending meetings, participating in events, or other activities, civic associations mediate the political participation of millions of Americans each year.

Yet, even within this group, degrees of participation can vary widely. Among the 79 percent who reported being involved in some association in the Citizen Participation Study, 35 percent had not attended any meetings of the association in the prior year, and 58 percent report being inactive members.[25] Among those who have titled leadership positions within the associations, participation levels can also vary widely. A 2003 study of elected leaders of the Sierra Club, a national environmental association, found that leaders spent between 15 minutes and 240 hours per month on Sierra Club activities.[26] Some leaders took the position seriously, treating it almost like a part-time (or, in some instances, a full-time) job, while others did little more than read a couple of emails or participate in one phone call each month. What explains these differences?

23. Verba, Schlozman, and Brady 1995, 62.

24. US Department of Commerce 2009.

25. Verba, Schlozman, and Brady 1995, 62.

26. Andrews, Ganz, Baggetta, Han, and Lim 2010; Baggetta, Han, and Andrews 2013.

DO THE ORGANIZATIONS MATTER? COMPARING HIGH- AND LOW-ENGAGEMENT CASES

Two vignettes describe the way organizational practices can interact with individual and contextual factors to explain differences in how involved people become.

Vignette 1: Danielle

Danielle is an internist who, in her own words, grew up in an "apolitical" family and had "little prior involvement" in politics. While in college, she took a class that forced her to participate in a local campaign "that I did a little bit of almost nothing on." She says, "I've always voted but I've never been that politically active." In 2004, while in medical school, a friend invited her to a party to watch then Senator Barack Obama's speech at the Democratic National Convention. Not knowing who he was, Danielle attended the party to socialize with her friends—but was inspired by the speech she heard. Afterwards, she signed up to be on Obama's mailing list and followed Obama's rapid political ascent. At the same time, she finished medical school and moved to a new community to start her residency and her career as a physician.

Although she followed news about Obama's presidential campaign throughout 2008, Danielle initially took no action with the campaign. One day, however, a colleague who knew Danielle supported Obama stopped her in the clinic and asked her to sign a petition of doctors who were supporting Obama. "It said doctors and it said Obama and I was for both." So Danielle signed the petition, thereby getting onto the mailing list of the National Association of Doctors. In the last month of the campaign, Danielle began to get more involved, making calls for Obama from the local campaign office. At first, she was apprehensive about doing this kind of work, but once she became friends with the other people in the office, she started going in every night after work. Then Obama carried his campaign to victory in a historic election.

Danielle finished the campaign inspired and exhilarated by the work she had done and wanted to stay involved with politics. At that time, the National Association of Doctors seemed like her best option. She went to the National Association of Doctors website and indicated that she would be interested in getting more involved. Soon, leaders of the association reached out to her, asking her to take on more and more leadership responsibilities. She progressively got more involved but, as Danielle puts it, she got really hooked one weekend when she was doing some work for the association. They were engaged in a big petition campaign and needed someone to take names from the petition and enter them into a large database. Danielle agreed to do it, spending the whole weekend entering data on more than 700 people. She "got really into it," and began emailing some of the people on the list, to find out more about where they lived and what they do. She realized that "behind each name was a real person. That's when I got really committed." As she got to know more of the people involved in the association, Danielle progressively took on more and more leadership responsibility and is now a national leader of the National Association of Doctors.

Vignette 2: Donna

Donna has a different story. She immigrated with her parents to the United States when she was 15 and became interested in and active in politics when she became a naturalized citizen. As a medical student, she became a campus leader with respect to progressive health politics. During the 2008 election, Donna was active in a number of student organizations, including being president of her campus American Medical Student Association (AMSA) chapter, and very involved in an organization dedicated to global health issues. Because her medical school was located in a battleground state, she was recruited to become active with the local Obama campaign in 2008. Through this activity, she became involved with the National Association of Doctors, although she cannot remember precisely how she got onto their email list. "I think I received an email because I am registered as a Barack Obama supporter," she said.

When asked what her initial impressions of the National Association of Doctors were, she said, "I got email from [the National Association of Doctors] and we had a couple of our faculty members [at my medical school] who were members, so I definitely wanted to join." She liked the way emails from the National Association of Doctors helped her make sense of the complicated politics around health reform in 2009. "[Once] the Town Hall meetings [in August of 2009] were getting so chaotic, I wanted something that was a little more, what can I say? [The National Association of Doctors was] sort of sensible and good at explaining what was happening that made sense and was logical." She liked the National Association of Doctors because people she trusted were part of the association, and they provided her with information that she found useful.

Aside from receiving emails, however, Donna never became more involved. "From the moment I signed on, my activity really remained the same." She says she would have "loved to be more involved" but was never able to find the time to do so. When asked whether her expectations of the National Association of Doctors had been met, she said, "I can definitely appreciate the email updates from all the [National Association of Doctors] members and how they are doing…. I just wish there were more local events so I could meet other members of the organization." When asked about whether there are other people in her area who are active, Donna says, "I know there are other people," but she does not know them.

How do associational practices and behaviors affect the levels of activism and leadership members are willing to take on? Donna and Danielle took two different pathways into activism and had different reactions to the National Association of Doctors. While Danielle became increasingly involved with the association, Donna did not. What were the factors that influenced their choices to get more involved—or not?

Certainly their personal backgrounds and the broader context influenced their choices to become active in politics more generally. Donna was heavily influenced by her immigrant background, and Danielle's entry into political activity depended on a happenstance invite to a party she received from a friend in medical school. Danielle's life circumstances also affected her ability to get involved—it happened that the 2008

Obama campaign coincided with the end of her residency and she had time to devote to public activity. The larger political context also affected both women. Both Donna and Danielle's first important experience of politics came during the 2008 Obama campaign, and they were swept up in the tide of optimism and hope that came with electing the country's first African American president. Both individual and contextual factors affected Donna and Danielle's choices to get involved.

Their political involvement was not, however, just an accident of biography or political context. Organizational factors also mattered. Danielle's activism in the campaign became a commitment to long-term civic leadership when she began to recognize the value in the community of people represented by National Association of Doctors. Not all associations could have done that. The National Association of Doctors fostered a particular sense of collegiality and warmth that drew Danielle to it and kept her hooked. Donna, however, never experienced that sense of community. She appreciated the information that the National Association of Doctors provided her, but she wished they had more "local events" so that she could get to know other people. Donna's activism within the National Association of Doctors never escalated in the same way Danielle's did.

Donna's and Danielle's activism (or lack thereof) was not a foregone conclusion when they joined the association. Danielle could have tried to get more involved with National Association of Doctors after the 2008 election and found an association that lacked the social community she sought. Instead, Danielle had positive experiences with the National Association of Doctors, thus increasing her commitment to further activism within the association. Donna, on the other hand, had a history of being willing to take on activism and leadership, but never committed to doing so within the National Association of Doctors. She could have joined the National Association of Doctors, found a community of faculty and other medical students who cultivated her commitment to the association, and decided to shift some of her activism from AMSA to the National Association of Doctors. Instead, she never became more involved.

To understand how the National Association of Doctors made a difference in Donna's and Danielle's trajectories, we need to rule out other possibilities first. Perhaps that is just an artifact of the way Donna and

Danielle tell their stories. Thus, the first phase of this study consisted of a mixed-method, longitudinal set of comparative case studies designed to generate a rich, textured sense of the strategies civic associations use to engage activists. By comparing matched pairs of high-engagement chapters to low-engagement chapters, I was able to see what differentiated chapters that were particularly strong at mobilizing members from their peer chapters. To examine organizational practices within these chapters, I conducted longitudinal surveys with members, interviews with chapter leaders and volunteers, and ethnographic observations.

The first phase thus compared sub-organizational units within two different national civic associations (depicted in table 2-3). This phase examined local organizations (referred to throughout the book as a "chapter," "entity," "local," or "site"). To identify local chapters for inclusion in the study, I drew on association data indicating that certain regions are more effective than others in generating participation among their members. Within each national association, I identified three regions that are high-engagement, in terms of their ability to generate participation among members, and three regions that are low-engagement. I selected the cases in pairs, so that one high-engagement area was matched with one low-engagement area.

In matching the pairs of high- and low-engagement sites, I tried to anticipate other possible explanations for why certain sites are better at engaging people than other sites. Much previous research indicates that varied rates of activism and leadership within civic associations can be a function of the kind of people who join the association or the community within which the association works (see Appendix for further discussion of this research and for more detail on the process of case selection). In identifying the matched pairs, I wanted to account for these differences as much as possible by matching cases in terms of (a) the individual characteristics of the people who joined, and (b) the contextual characteristics of the communities in which they operated. By matching local chapters on these characteristics, I sought to minimize the possibility that differences in rates of engagement could be explained by differences in who joined or where the chapter operated.

Table 2-3. Phase I Research Design

The National Associations
(called "associations")

	National Association of Doctors		People for the Environment	
	HIGH-ENGAGEMENT ↔	LOW-ENGAGEMENT	HIGH-ENGAGEMENT ↔	LOW-ENGAGEMENT
Phase I unit of analysis: comparative case studies of local organizations (called "locals," "sites," or "chapters")	Greenville ↔	Clinton	Fairview ↔	Madison
	Springfield ↔	Bristol	Milton ↔	Marion
	Franklin ↔	Salem	Oxford ↔	Jackson
Activists and leaders	Names starting with "D"		Names starting with "P"	

NOTE: As discussed further in the Appendix, the names of the associations and the place names in the table above are disguised to protect their anonymity. Each of the matched pairs of high-engagement and low-engagement organizations were selected to minimize demographic, political, and civic differences between the two communities.

Table 2-4 compares the high-engagement sites in both the National Association of Doctors and People for the Environment to their low-engagement counterparts on a number of civic, political, and demographic characteristics. All of these data are discussed in more detail in Appendix. Suffice it to say here that two key points emerge from this comparison of the contextual and community characteristics: (1) all the high-engagement sites have historically higher levels of activism than their low-engagement counterparts, and (2) while civic, political, and demographic differences between the matched pairs exist, they are not systematic enough to explain the consistent differences in levels of engagement. For instance, in some cases the communities in which the low-engagement chapters operated were more affluent, while in others the communities of the high-engagement chapters were. In some cases, the communities where the low-engagement chapters worked were more politically liberal, while in other cases the communities of the high-engagement chapters were. No two communities are perfectly matched to each other. The data in table 2-4, however, show that there is no consistent pattern of differences between these communities that could explain the disparities in engagement that emerge.

COMPARING NEW MEMBERS

What about the people who join these chapters? What if the relative abilities of chapters to engage more members in activism reflect differences in the kinds of people who join in high-engagement locations and the kinds of people who join in low-engagement locations? To examine these differences, I conducted a study of new members.

National Association of Doctors

In March and April 2010, I conducted a study of new members of the six National Association of Doctors study sites. I sent mail and email surveys to 147 members who had just joined the association. Seventy-two

Table 2-4. Comparison of Matched Pairs of High- and Low-Engagement Sites in Terms of Rates of Activism, Measures of Civic and Political Context, and Demographics

Difference between High- and Low-Engagement (High-Low)

Indicator	NATIONAL ASSOCIATION OF DOCTORS			PEOPLE FOR THE ENVIRONMENT		
	FAIRVIEW-MADISON	MILTON-MARION	OXFORD-JACKSON	GREENVILLE-CLINTON	SPRINGFIELD-BRISTOL	FRANKLIN-SALEM
Measures of Activism						
% Activist (Oct 2010)[a]	4.3	4.7	14.0	16.3	16.8	6.8
Measures of Civic and Political Context						
General civic culture						
Number of civic groups (NCCS 2003 data)	−580	231	−363	−85	−68	234
Political orientation						
Mean Democratic presidential vote in 2000, 2004, 2008 (percentage point difference)	−2.4	4.2	0.7	0.1	−0.1	−0.1
Medical Culture (data from Dartmouth Atlas)						
All physicians per 100,000 residents	16	32	10			
PCPs per 100,000 residents	8	12	2			
Acute care hospital beds per 1,000 residents	0	0	0			
% Patients giving high hospital rating (2007)	−3	2	−4			

(Continued)

Table 2-4 (CONTINUED)

Difference between High- and Low-Engagement (High-Low)

Indicator	NATIONAL ASSOCIATION OF DOCTORS			PEOPLE FOR THE ENVIRONMENT		
	FAIRVIEW-MADISON	MILTON-MARION	OXFORD-JACKSON	GREENVILLE-CLINTON	SPRINGFIELD-BRISTOL	FRANKLIN-SALEM
Environmental Indicators						
ACEEE State Scorecard (2009)				15.5	-16	.5
Green Index				-3	-2	12
Number of environmental groups per capita				6,705	-2,237	12,152
Demographics (Census data)						
Total population	-242,355	-912,439	587,465	1,608,515	-5,157,472	14,809,540
Median household income (2008 inflation-adjusted dollars)	1,509	-7,106	-3,471	660	-695	2,971
% High school graduate or higher	1.7	6.1	5.9	0.0	3.0	-4.0
Race: % white	3.6	39.7	7.9	-3.0	12.0	1.0
% Foreign born	4.2	16.3	1.5	2.0	-9.0	9.0

[a] Rates of activism are calculated based on internal organizational data, using organizational definitions of what constitutes activism (see text). Data sources discussed in the appendix.

respondents returned their surveys for a 49 percent response rate, which was relatively evenly divided between high-performing (38 surveys) and low-performing sites (34 surveys). From the survey, I was able to develop a picture of the kinds of people who join the National Association of Doctors and the reasons they joined in different locations.

Because the study is focused on comparing differences between high-engagement and low-engagement groups, it is important to examine differences between people from each of those groups to see if high-engagement groups are attracting different kinds of people than low-engagement groups. Table 2-5 compares respondents from high-engagement and low-engagement groups on demographic and political dimensions. Across all three of these graphs, there do not appear to be any significant initial differences between people who join the high-engagement groups and those who join the low-engagement groups.

On demographic dimensions, table 2-5 shows that across gender, race, marital status, the percentage of respondents with children, education, and mobility, there are no statistically significant differences between respondents from high- and low-engagement groups. The one area in which they appear to differ is age, with respondents from high-engagement groups (average age = 44.8 years old) being slightly older than respondents from low-engagement groups (average age = 38.6 years old). The difference is only significant at $p < 0.1$.

On self-reported political orientations, table 2-5 again shows no significant differences. Self-reported levels of political interest, efficacy, and extremism of political views are commonly used as measures of people's political motivation.[27] People with higher levels of political interest and efficacy, and more extreme political views, are thought to be more motivated to participate in politics. Respondents from high- and low-engagement groups, however, showed no statistically significant differences on any of these dimensions. Respondents from low-engagement groups were as likely to report being interested in politics and to feel that they had a voice in politics as respondents from high-engagement groups.

27. e.g., Schlozman 2003; Verba, Schlozman, and Brady 1995; Rosenstone and Hansen 1993.

Table 2-5. COMPARISON OF NEW MEMBERS IN LOW- AND HIGH-ENGAGEMENT
SITES IN THE NATIONAL ASSOCIATION OF DOCTORS

	Low-Engagement Sites	High-Engagement Sites
Demographics		
% Female	55	45
% White	73	61
% Married	64	55
% with no children at home	75	62
% Completed training	55	67
Mean age[†]	38.6	44.8
Mean number of years living in present town	9.3	12.4
Political Orientations		
Liberal-Conservative	4.7	4.9
Political interest	3.3	3.3
Political efficacy	2.9	2.8
Previous Political Activity		
Discuss politics	3.9	3.7
Work with others to solve community problems	2.6	2.8
Contact public official	2.4	2.5
Contact newspaper or magazine	1.7	1.9
Call in to radio or TV	1.2	1.2
Attend speech[†]	2.3	2.7
Take part in protest	1.7	1.9
Sign a petition[*]	3	3.4
Volunteer for a campaign	1.9	1.8
Boycott products	2.9	2.8
Buycott products	3.1	3
Buttons, stickers, signs	2.5	2.3
Donate $	3	3.1
Vote	4.5	4.6
Total number of civic groups	3.3	3.6

[†] $p < 0.1$ [*] $p < 0.05$ See tables A-1 and A-2 and discussion in the appendix for more details on the scaling of these variables.

Finally, table 2-5 compares respondents on previous participation in civic and political activity. On most activities, there are no statistically significant differences between respondents from high- and low-engagement sites. Respondents from low-engagement sites are as likely as respondents from high-engagement sites to report discussing politics with others; working with others to solve community problems; contacting public officials or the media; taking part in protests; volunteering for campaigns; boycotting or buying products from companies as a political statement; displaying political buttons, stickers, or signs; donating money; voting; or joining other civic groups. Respondents from high-engagement groups were more likely to report engaging in two types of activities: attending a speech, informal seminar, or teach-in about politics (difference significant at $p < 0.1$) and signing a petition (difference significant at $p < .05$). While this may provide some mild evidence that respondents from high-engagement groups are more active than respondents from low-engagement groups, the fact that no differences appeared in 13 out of 15 activities on the list (and no differences appeared in overall levels of political motivation) leads me to believe that there is something else happening. Perhaps some proportion of the differences between these groups can be explained on the basis of the different kinds of people they attract, but it is hard to believe that all the differences are due to those factors— given that the respondents from low-engagement groups are so similar to respondents from high-engagement groups on most demographic and political dimensions.

People for the Environment

I also sent a survey to members who had first joined People for the Environment between January and March 2010. The mail survey was sent to 3,142 people in June 2010, and 692 returned them for a 22 percent response rate (one reminder email was sent). The respondents were evenly divided between high-engagement sites (367 surveys returned) and low-engagement sites (325 surveys returned). The survey asked people about their demographic backgrounds, their previous civic and political activity and interests, their early experiences with People for the Environment, and their reasons for joining. From the survey, I was able to draw a picture of the kinds of people joining People for the Environment.

In comparing the characteristics of new members, it is particularly important to examine individual characteristics that are known to be predictive of participation. The dominant model of political participation predicts that there are three major factors associated with participation: resources, recruitment, and motivation.[28] People are more likely to participate if they have the resources necessary for participation (such as free time, knowledge, civic skills, etc.), if they are motivated to participate (political interest and efficacy), and if someone recruits them. The two main individual-level factors, thus, are resources and motivation.

Table 2-6 compares respondents from high- and low-engagement sites on the resources and demographic characteristics commonly associated with participation. Although a few small differences emerge, there are not large enough systematic differences across the two groups to warrant the conclusion that differences in individual resources explains differences in engagement across these groups. The kinds of new members that high- and low-engagement groups are attracting are comparable in terms of the percent who are married, the percent with children at home, levels of education, the percent working full-time, average income, and the average number of years living in their present town. The survey also asked new members to identify the kinds of skills that they practice in the workplace or other parts of their life, to capture the kinds of civic skills these individuals are developing. Comparing the two groups shows that members from low-engagement groups report developing approximately the same number of civic skills as members from high-engagement groups. Small differences do emerge in terms of race, gender, and age. Both groups have very few minorities joining, but low-engagement groups are statistically likely to have more members who are white (a difference of 5 percentage points, statistically significant at $p < .05$), female (a difference of 5 percentage points, significant at

28. Verba, Schlozman, and Brady 1995; Schlozman 2003.

Table 2-6. Comparison of New Members in Low- and High-Engagement Sites in People for the Environment

	Low-Engagement Sites	High-Engagement Sites
Demographics		
% Female[†]	55	50
% White[*]	93	88
% Married	48	48
% with no children at home	85	83
% Graduate education	50	47
% Working full-time	39	44
Mean income	3.4	3.5
Mean number of civic skills	6.1	6.1
Mean age[†]	54.8	52.8
Mean number of years living in present town	17.8	18.6
Political Orientations		
Liberal-Conservative	5.1	5.0
Political interest	4.1	4.0
Political efficacy	2.5	2.4
Previous Political Activity		
Discuss politics[*]	3.6	3.5
Work with others to solve community problems	2.5	2.4
Contact public official	2.4	2.4
Contact newspaper or magazine	1.8	1.8
Call in to radio or TV	1.3	1.3
Attend speech	2.1	2.1
Take part in protest[*]	1.6	1.7
Sign a petition[*]	3.1	2.9
Volunteer for a campaign	1.8	1.8
Boycott products	2.9	2.9
Buttons, stickers, signs	2.4	2.3
Donate $	2.7	2.6
Vote	3.8	3.7
Total number of civic groups	9.9	9.9

[†] $p < 0.1$ [*]$p < 0.05$ See tables A-1 and A-2 and discussion in the appendix for more details on the scaling of these variables.

p <.1), and slightly older (a difference of two years, statistically significant at p <.1). Interestingly, the differences do not move in the direction one would expect. In general, research finds that non-minorities, women, and slightly older people are more likely to be active in politics—yet, in this sample, the high-engagement groups are attracting more minorities, fewer women, and slightly younger people. Thus, it seems unlikely that these small demographic differences account for differences in activism between high- and low-engagement groups.

Table 2-6 also compares respondents from high- and low-engagement groups along dimensions commonly used to measure motivation. Specifically, I examine levels of political interest, efficacy, liberalism, and previous political activity. As with the comparison of resources, while small differences between the groups exist, they do not seem large enough to fully explain differences in levels of activism between the groups. In terms of self-reported levels of motivation, the groups are virtually identical in levels of political interest, efficacy, and ideological extremity (liberalism). The two groups are also very similar in their reported levels of engagement in working with others to solve community problems; contacting public officials or media; attending political speeches, teach-ins, or other educational events; volunteering for campaigns; boycotting (or buying) products from companies whose political stances they dislike (or favor); displaying political buttons, campaigns, or signs; donating money; voting; and affiliating with civic groups. There are statistically significant (at p <.05) differences between the two groups in terms of discussing politics, taking part in protests, and signing petitions. Respondents from low-engagement groups are more slightly likely to discuss politics and sign petitions, while respondents from high-engagement groups are slightly more likely to have taken part in a protest in the past two years. Participating in protests is a much more intensive form of activism than discussing politics or signing petitions, in that it is more time-consuming, requires people to leave their home, and, in some cases, can involve some risk. Thus, the differences between the two groups in protest activity may signal that members from high-engagement groups have a slightly higher propensity to engage in more intensive forms of activism. The fact that those differences do not emerge in any other activities, even those that are intensive (such as attending speeches or volunteering for a campaign), leads me to believe that further investigation into the differences between these two groups is warranted.

The new member survey thus provides a profile of the kinds of people who join People for the Environment in the six sites. Because it was conducted shortly after these members joined the association, it captures their demographic, civic, and political characteristics before they have had much interaction with People for the Environment. In examining this information, I find that the kinds of people who are joining low-engagement groups do not seem to be systematically different from the kinds of people joining high-engagement groups. On most individual characteristics correlated with higher rates of participation, the two groups are statistically indistinguishable. The small differences that do exist may explain some portion of the variance in engagement between the two types of groups, but they do not seem to capture the full story. As a result, these findings lay the groundwork for a further investigation into the organizational differences between high- and low-engagement sites.

LEVELS OF ENGAGEMENT IN HIGH- AND LOW-ENGAGEMENT CHAPTERS AFTER ONE YEAR

How did the people in these high- and low-engagement sites differ in their levels of engagement after one year? As previously described, I selected local chapters from People for the Environment and the National Association of Doctors for the study based partly on the historic rates of activism they were able to sustain. I then surveyed the new members joining the chapters and found that new members joining high- and low-engagement chapters did not differ from each other when they first joined. Nonetheless, I found there were significant differences between the two groups after one year of membership in People for the Environment and National Association of Doctors.

In People for the Environment, members of high-engagement chapters were significantly more likely to have engaged in offline action than members of low-engagement chapters. Figure 2-7 shows participation

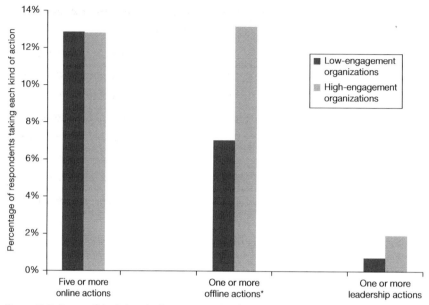

Figure 2-7. Rates of Activism in Low- versus High-Engagement Sites after One Year of Membership in People for the Environment (*p < .05)

rates in three forms of action (online, offline, and leadership) in People for the Environment after one year of membership (leadership actions are actions in which the person took responsibility for a clear outcome). There were no statistically significant differences between high- and low-engagement chapters in the percentage of people who participated in online activity. People in high-engagement chapters, however, were significantly more likely to have participated in two or more offline actions. In addition, although the differences were not statistically significant (because of the low number of people overall who took leadership action), people from high-engagement groups were twice as likely as people from low-engagement groups to have taken leadership actions.

The lack of difference between high- and low-engagement chapters in terms of online actions is telling about the differences between mobilizing and organizing. Mobilizers have a much easier time engaging people in online action than in offline action. Because chapters can cheaply and easily send requests for online action, they can generate participation by designing a request they believe is attractive enough for people to respond to and sending the request to large numbers of people. The fact that high- and low-engagement chapters did not differ in terms of their ability to engage online actions indicates similarities in their ability to build their lists and design attractive asks. They all engaged in mobilizing activity, and the ability to do so did not differentiate them from each other.

The differences between the People for the Environment chapters, in-stead, emerged in their ability to engage people in offline activity. Getting people to a face-to-face meeting requires more cultivation of their ac-tivism than does getting them to respond to an online request for action. While low- and high-engagement chapters were similar in their rates of prompting online action, high-engagement chapters had consistently higher rates of offline actions. This difference paints a picture of the im-portance of cultivating people for activism.

In the National Association of Doctors, the differences between low- and high-engagement chapters were also clear. As shown in figure 2-8, members of high-engagement chapters were statistically significantly more likely to participate in online and offline action. The National Association of Doctors defines "activists" within the organization as those

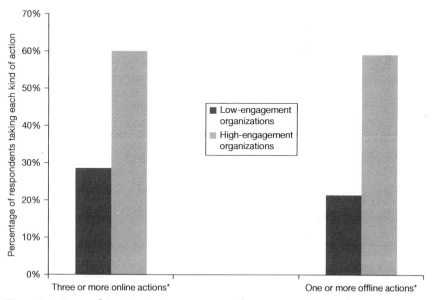

Figure 2-8. Rates of Activism in Low- versus High-Engagement Sites after One Year of Membership in the National Association of Doctors (*p < .05)

who participate in three or more online actions or any offline action. On both of these dimensions, statistically significant differences between low- and high-engagement chapters are apparent.

The ability of high-engagement chapters in the National Association of Doctors to engage repeated participation again shows the importance of cultivation of activism. Both low- and high-engagement chapters were able to design activities and asks that would get people to participate once, or even twice. Once people participated, however, getting them to come back was a different challenge. Here, high-engagement chapters that relied more on organizing strategies differentiated themselves.

SO WHAT DOES THIS ALL MEAN?

The data in this chapter show that although some individual and contextual differences exist between the high- and low-engagement sites in the study, the patterns are not clear enough nor are the differences large enough to explain all the differences in engagement levels. No pair of local chapters is exactly the same, but an examination of community data on the pairs of high- and low-engagement chapters in the study revealed no clear patterns that might explain the different levels of activism. Some high-engagement chapters operated in more politically liberal communities than their low-engagement counterparts, while others did not. As table 2-3 shows, some high-engagement chapters worked in more populous areas, while others did not. Some high-engagement chapters worked in areas with a denser civic culture, while others did not. Likewise, a comparison of the kinds of people joining the local chapters in these areas showed that they did not differ from each other in systematic ways. People joining high-engagement chapters were not more politically interested, efficacious, or involved than those joining low-engagement chapters.

Put together, these findings seem to imply that other factors have the potential to make a powerful difference in how engaged members become. What are those factors? What are the differences in organizational practice? Given that high-engagement chapters are not operating in communities in which it is easier to organize or to draw members more poised for political action, how are they better able to engage activists and cultivate leaders?

Previous research on the relationship between associations (and movements) and participation examines multiple ways that associations can facilitate participation. Associations can help shape social-psychological factors, such as a sense of shared identity or individual and collective agency.[29] Associations can also frame participatory opportunities in ways that make participation meaningful,[30] shape social interactions and recruitment drives that facilitate participation,[31] and shape incentives for participation.[32] They can also create "high-quality" interpersonal interactions within the organization that can make commitment more likely.[33] This research shows that associational practices can make a difference—subsequent chapters describe how these pieces come together into divergent strategies for engagement.

29. Collective identity refers to "a shared sense of one-ness or we-ness anchored in real or imagined shared attributes and experiences" (Snow 2001, 2213). See Polletta and Jasper 2001; Bandura 1997; Snow and Soule 2010; Kanter 1972; Teske 1997b.

30. Snow 2007; Snow and Benford 1988.

31. Rosenstone and Hansen 1993; Gerber and Green 2000; Green and Gerber 2004; Verba, Schlozman, and Brady 1995; Nickerson 2006, 2008; Arceneaux 2007; Gerber, Green, and Larimer 2008.

32. e.g., Wilson 1973.

33. Klein, Becker, and Meyer 2009, 254, 260.

3

Choosing Strategies for Building Power

Civic associations always have more things they could do than they have time to do. There are always more decision-makers to influence; more legislative, legal, political, or advocacy opportunities available; more money to raise; more people to engage; and more leaders to develop. Given this constant pressure on their resources, associations have to choose how best to allocate resources to achieve their goals. Where should they spend their time, money, and effort?

In a world of constrained resources, civic associations dedicate resources to whatever they think helps them build their power. Sometimes, the work may involve organizing, sometimes mobilizing and sometimes neither. Constantly faced with another advocacy opportunity on the horizon, association leaders often prioritize writing a policy report, planning the next event, or networking with decision-makers over putting time into mobilizing people for action, or developing the capacity of volunteers to engage in further activism and leadership. Particularly for associations interested in doing deep, transformational organizing is the question of whether they can do it in such a way that enables them to get to scale. Can they do the transformational work of organizing and still achieve the breadth of engagement they desire?

Given all of these considerations, how do associations decide what will be most effective in helping them build power? Multiple factors affect whether associations perceive that acting as lone wolves, mobilizing, or organizing helps them build power. How associations choose their goals and decide what kinds of strategies are most effective for achieving those goals depends on a complex combination of circumstances and resources external and internal to the association, as well as the perspectives of the individuals making those choices, and the histories and structures of the association itself. The complexity of the decision-making environment in which leaders work often makes it hard to clearly identify all of the strategic choices—like mobilizing and organizing—that are available. This chapter describes how some of these factors come together as leaders make strategic choices about how to engage people. I examine the way external conditions, interpretive frames, and organizational structures are related to the strategic choices chapters made about how to engage people. High-engagement chapters distinguish themselves from their low-engagement counterparts by creating a strategy in which getting their work done depends on engaging others as activists and leaders. The strategy for accomplishing their public goals, in other words, is integrated with a distributed leadership structure. I discuss how that strategy emerged from pressures felt from the external environment, stories that people within the chapter told about what those pressures were and how to respond to them, and choices about how to structure responsibility to meet external challenges. I look particularly at the distributed leadership structures that organizers adopt as a way of reconciling the twin demands of breadth and depth. Two vignettes provide a glimpse into this process.

TWO VIGNETTES

Vignette 1: Transitioning from Mobilizing to Organizing

Priscilla, who leads one of the high-engagement chapters in People for the Environment, describes her work:

> Yeah, well, I think about when I first started in [People for the Environment]. There was so much going on in [our state]: we're fighting

[lots of energy fights], there's all these clean energy possibilities, there's just everything happening all the time. We're having all these public meetings and town halls and we're organizing locally to build volunteer groups. We're having town halls all the time and press conferences trying to generate media. I was spending my time traveling around the state organizing all these events. I was having volunteers fill different roles, but I was the point person that everybody was looking to. My gut was that we need volunteers—not me—to be organizing these things. I don't really have the capacity to be traveling around all over the state…. And so [if I'm] going from one thing to the next to the next and just traveling all around the state, there's very little time. And the intention wasn't really there to have like those one-on-one meetings consistently, and identify prospects, and recruit leaders. And the structure wasn't there to plug people into a volunteer role because they all needed a lot of my time to take on those roles and I didn't have time.

Priscilla describes how she attended a training run by the national People for the Environment association, which introduced her to principles of organizing. Once she began to see the difference between "organizing events" and "organizing organizers," she began to talk to other leaders within her local People for the Environment chapter to see if they could reorient their work toward organizing. As a team, they made a decision to shift toward organizing.

One of the things that has become really clear to me is that one of the key challenges we face is that the structure within [People for the Environment] is oftentimes as organizers we're organizing these events. And we go from event to event to event. Which keeps us very busy especially here [in our state] because there are huge challenges that we're facing…. As organizers, if we're going event by event, then it's a problem because then there's always another event we have to do. And the organizers can't focus on the people. It's so difficult to keep people engaged and there's all these amazing people that come out to these events.

    And so instead, we need to be organizing organizers instead of organizing events. That is what is going to help us to build our capacity and we aren't doing that. Instead we should be organizing teams of volunteers who are organizing the events. And so that's what we're doing now. We're always identifying, finding leaders, and plugging them into these teams around the state. So that's what we've been working on for the past six months and it's been really great.

Vignette 2: The Lone Wolves

Paul, a leader in one of the low-engagement chapters in People for the Environment, describes his work:

In the last ten years, at least talking from [our] perspective, we are in trouble because we are losing membership, just like lots of people, and we are losing the ability to get people to work on stuff…. Yes and I am one of them, we all become lone wolves…. There are different types of people with different skills. I am not a very good organizer. I have tried and tried and tried. I have been involved with the [association] since 1976, so for 34 years. But in my efforts to get people organized and involved, I have found that I am deficient [and our whole organization is deficient]. So I dive in and I do stuff, but getting other people motivated to do stuff is hard—not even the stuff I do, but simpler stuff…. My perspective is that we rarely find those people [who will do stuff] and then when we find them, we lose those people [because we burn them out] and it is very difficult to replace them…. So we have had a lot of turnover of people and we haven't had a plan in place, a way to replace those people. A volunteer recruitment, training, retention and anti-burnout program.

Like I said, unfortunately nowadays what I do is mostly individual. I [work to protect forests and wildlife preserves in my area]. Basically, I kind of comment on in an administrative fashion and interact with those agents—that's the US Wildlife Service, National Park Service and US Forest on forestry issues…. And we have a lawsuit and we have fought this [new parkway] for 25 years. So I do that and I do some other transportation stuff. I consider myself the utility guy. A lot of times I will see something and we don't have anyone to cover it and I will cover it…. So that is the problem. One person doing too many things.

Most of my work has been lobbying those administrative agencies and trying to be a watchdog or provide some sort of citizen oversight. I want them to think [People for the Environment] is everywhere. That is one of my basic strategies of sitting in the audience. At any rate I wish there were—what I would like to do is clone myself and have half a dozen other people doing something because there are a lot of meetings that don't get attended, and then there are a lot of meetings that someone else will go to that I should. I am very aware of my situation, and ultimately even though I do good work, and I will be happy to send you some of my work if you want to look at it, it is not the best thing. There aren't many people who read big technical documents. I am one of those people. I read the EIS and I make voluminous comments. So that is my forte, and I also like to feel like because I have been around for so long I have some ideas about strategy and things like that. But one person can only do so much.

In the descriptions of their own work, Priscilla and Paul summarize many of the advantages and challenges of adopting an organizing approach, in which they focus on developing the capacity of others to take on leadership, versus other approaches. Although Paul recognized the need for and importance of trying to develop others as activists and leaders, he felt unable to do it and ended up working, in his own words, as a "lone wolf." Because many people within his chapter acted as lone wolves, people who did take on leadership often burned out from carrying too much weight on their shoulders. In addition, he always felt that he did not have enough people to do the kind of work he wanted to do. Even though Paul pursued primarily insider strategies, he did not have enough people who could attend administrative hearings or participate in lobbying the bureaucratic agents.

Priscilla led a local affiliate of People for the Environment that had been focused on mobilizing, but was transitioning toward organizing because they felt like it would help them achieve the scale they desired. Her chapter was making this switch because they were frustrated by the time their leaders were spending organizing events, instead of developing the engagement of people who came to those events. She makes a distinction between "organizing events" and "organizing organizers." When the leaders were focused on "organizing events," the immediate demands of putting together the next event drove the leader's time, forcing the leaders to be constantly reactive to the pace of the event schedule. They were not able to focus on maintaining the engagement of people who attended those events or be more proactive in their broader strategy—creating a self-reinforcing cycle. The leader would put an enormous amount of time into planning an event and getting enough people to attend it, and then would be unable to invest in developing relationships with those people or cultivating their activism. Without any cultivation, the activism of those people who came to the first event would stagnate or flag. When the leader then needed to generate attendance for her next event, she had to start virtually anew. To break out of this cycle, Priscilla was trying to transition her chapter toward "organizing organizers" where the leaders would focus their energy on developing teams of people who were invested with the responsibility of putting events together. Ideally, the leader would develop the capacity of more people to take on responsibility within the chapter, thereby increasing the capacity of the chapter to get more work done by simultaneously putting on events and cultivating the activism of others. Priscilla's chapter decided, in other words, that to get to scale, they needed to go deep first. Developing leaders would allow them to achieve the breadth they needed.

The distinctions that Priscilla and Paul make between lone wolves, mobilizing, and organizing exemplify the complicated choices associations make about how to build power. How associations interpret the world around them and structure their work, the choices they make about what strategy to pursue, and the levels of engagement they are able to sustain are all interrelated. This chapter explores those interrelationships, focusing particularly on the way that the high-engagement chapters became organizers.

UNDERSTANDING THE STRATEGIC CHOICE TO MOBILIZE OR ORGANIZE

How do chapters choose whether and when to mobilize or organize? The decision to mobilize or organize is a strategic choice about how to develop and deploy organizational resources. Organizing is hard. When done well, it can yield high numbers of activists and leaders, but it takes a lot of resources. Civic associations have to put a lot of time, energy, and effort into getting people to commit their precious time to activism, and to developing leaders who can take responsibility for outcomes. Organizing on a large scale is even harder. Often, the value of investing all of these resources in organizing is unclear. When an association can achieve its objectives through mobilizing or lone wolf strategies, it often will.

Understanding how local chapters make this decision depends on understanding in general how strategic choices are made. Sometimes the process of developing strategy is conceptualized as a relatively rational process, in which an association faces a challenge, researches the political opportunity structure, identifies a range of alternative choices to meet the challenge, carefully evaluates each alternative, and then chooses the optimal path. In this conceptualization, the strategic process seems to have a rationality that rises above the messiness of any association's day-to-day operations.

Strategic decision-making in the associations I studied was more dependent on the context from which the need emerged. The strategic choice about whether and when to mobilize or organize was interrelated with the associational context, the inclinations of the individuals within the association, and structural choices made in the past that defined the path the association was on. A combination of external and internal factors and resources influenced the strategic choices the associations perceived and made.

In their studies of contentious politics, Charles Tilly and his colleagues argue that the strategic choices that movement actors make depend on the changing nature and scope of political authority, and the available technology.[1] He argues that repertoires of contentious politics in the eighteenth and nineteenth centuries were more "particular, in that participants were drawn from a limited geographic area, protests addressed local actors or elites, [and] the tactics were specific to the grievances." Protest activities included things like "grain seizures, field invasions, barricades, and the use of music, irreverent costumes, and other performances that ridiculed local authorities."[2] As governments became larger and more centralized in the twentieth century, the geographic scale of the claims that associations would make increased. Technology enabled the development of new

1. Tilly 1978, 1986; McAdam, Tarrow, and Tilly 2001.

2. Taylor and Van Dyke 2007, 271.

strategic repertoires as well, as the ability of associations to reach ever widening groups of people emerged with the development of mass communications and the Internet. External conditions shape, in other words, the opportunities associations have to make their claims.

How association leaders interpret these external conditions depends on the internal culture and narratives. These narratives shape how people within the association interpret the challenges, opportunities, and choices it faces.[3] Francesca Polletta and James Jasper argue that strategic choices "reflect what we believe, what we are comfortable with, what we like, who we are."[4] Strategic choices are not purely instrumental assessments of opportunities and constraints, but are instead the product of individuals and associations interpreting and making meaning of the world around them. The choices that individuals and associations make are inevitably shaped by their own histories, past experiences, and past choices. These histories, experiences, and patterns of interpretation are all part of an association's culture or, as veteran organizer Marshall Ganz calls it, its narrative.[5] The strategic choices that I observed emerged out of this context. Strategizing was not done in a vacuum, but instead within a context that affected the way people within the association interpreted the problem, perceived the alternatives it had, and made choices about what path to take.

Once an association adopts an organizing approach, however, it has a certain path dependence—or "stickiness"—to it that makes it more likely that leaders in the future will continue to organize. The stickiness emerges from the way adopting an organizing approach influences the kinds of narratives leaders create to explain their success, the experiences of individuals who are making decisions about future strategies, and the kinds of structures that the association creates.[6] Once an association adopted

3. Snow and Benford 1988; Gamson 1992.

4. Polletta and Jasper 2001, 284.

5. Ganz 2010.

6. Ganz 2009.

an organizing approach, volunteer leaders were trained in organizing and began to think about investing in members and developing leaders as their core approach to achieving social change. They began to develop skills, experiences, and narratives that attributed their source of power to the people they were able to cultivate as activists and leaders. In addition, they created structures that made organizing possible. Thus, when future strategic dilemmas came before the association, the leaders asked themselves, "Where does our power originate?" and "What kind of resources do we have that we can use?" Given the experiences they had in the past, the answer was more likely to point to organizing.

HOW DO ORGANIZERS BECOME ORGANIZERS?

As Priscilla describes, reorienting a chapter toward an organizing approach is extremely time-intensive and often requires a fundamental shift in the way leaders spend their time and conceptualize their work. When done well, it can expand the power of the chapter, but it also can require a tremendous amount of organizational resources to develop the new structure. One question, then, is why do some chapters move in that direction while others do not? What drives chapters to move in that direction? Teasing out causality in situations like this is extremely challenging—for instance, do local chapters adopt an organizing approach because a national campaign forces them to do so, or do they choose to work on the national campaign because they can develop the organizing capacity? The non-linear process of adopting strategies within chapters further complicates attempts to pinpoint causal predictors. Instead of emerging linearly, strategy evolves from a series of overlapping conversations between individuals and groups, conversations that are contingent upon the chapter's resources, interpretive frames, existing structures, previous decisions, and other factors.

Although a precise causal story is impossible to tell, examination of the six high-engagement sites in this study reveals a pattern in which some exogenous challenge prompts the chapter to reconsider its approach to engaging people. The decision to organize in response to this challenge is linked to the individual and collective narratives within the local chapter, the chapter history and structures, its resources, and other factors that influence the choice to move toward organizing.

Exogenous Challenges

When asked about how they first adopted an organizing strategy, leaders from four of the six high-engagement sites in the study discussed external conditions that prompted the chapter to begin doing its work differently. External conditions—such as the pressures of working with a presidential campaign, large geographic areas that needed to be organized, or time pressures on existing leaders—created situations in which the leaders were not able to do their work alone. The exogenous challenges created a resource constraint (or abundance) within the chapter that forced leaders to reconsider their choices.

The external challenge that Priscilla faced was the sheer size of the geographic area she was expected to organize. She worked as part of the high-engagement site called Franklin in People for the Environment, and she was frustrated by her inability to do all the work that was needed to engage people across her entire geographic turf. Priscilla describes the challenge she faced:

> [The national advocacy department in People for the Environment] identified five places where we definitely needed to build activity because it was politically necessary for the campaign. These were places I had never gotten to before because I just didn't have time. So we needed more people to get there.

Priscilla was working in a state that was spread out geographically, and she simply could not cover all the areas necessary to achieve the political goals that People for the Environment had set for its campaign. This pressure acted as an exogenous challenge that forced Priscilla to reconsider her options for getting the work done.

In two other instances, the high-engagement chapters were located in battleground states in recent presidential elections, and this placed greater demand for activity on the People for the Environment and National Association of Doctors chapters. The high-engagement chapters Springfield (in People for the Environment) and Oxford (in the National Association of Doctors) were both located in battleground states, whereas their low-engagement counterparts were not. Being in a battleground state meant that the national association put more pressure on the local chapters to expand activity and to coordinate their work with the presidential campaigns. In addition, the mobilization that occurred through the presidential campaigns identified pools of people who could potentially be engaged in the work of the National Association of Doctors and People for the Environment. The dual pressures of being asked to do more work to support the campaign and the growing pool of prospective activists forced leaders in both chapters to realize they could not do the work by themselves.

Resource considerations can thus push associations in two different ways to consider organizing. On the one hand, resource constraints force leaders to find new ways to meet their goals, often by developing volunteer leadership. On the other hand, resource abundance can push also chapters toward organizing. When the high-engagement chapters faced an abundance of volunteers who had been mobilized through the presidential campaign, they had to get their leadership structure up to scale to meet the demands of keeping this group of people engaged. Thus, they began to invest in developing leaders.

Other high-engagement chapters had leaders with increasing time constraints. Many of the original leaders of the high-engagement chapter Milton in the National Association of Doctors were also on the national leadership team of the National Association of Doctors. As a result, their time was stretched between the demands of running the local chapter and the demands of participating in leadership at the national level.

In all of these instances, site leaders chose to respond by adopting an organizing strategy. Priscilla decided she needed "more people to get there." Lacking the ability to do the work alone, the leaders in the battleground states, out of sheer desperation, began to recruit and develop other volunteers to take on more leadership. In doing so, they inadvertently began to set up an organizing structure within the chapter that expanded the scope of what they could do. The chapter leaders who were unable to work at the local level because of their work at the national level alleviated time pressures by recruiting and developing other local leaders who could take on more responsibility in the local chapter. As they did so, they began to create a culture of leadership development that persisted even after they left. The new leaders who were brought in replicated the same process of recruiting, building relationships with, and developing other leaders that they had witnessed. As this practice was passed on from one generation of leaders to the next, it became more formalized and elaborated until it became a core part of the way the National Association of Doctors operated in this city.

The choice to organize in response to resource constraints, however, was not a foregone conclusion. Resource constraints (or abundance) alone are not enough to push an association toward an organizing model. It also requires leaders in the chapter to choose those strategies. One of the low-engagement sites in the National Association of Doctors, for instance, was also a battleground state in presidential elections, but did not adopt the same organizing approach that others did. Likewise, leaders of both of the chapters in the matched pair Franklin and Salem in People for the Environment faced resource constraints, as they were operating in geographically large states with large rural populations. The core group of leaders was not able to cover the entire state very easily, and they found it particularly difficult to generate participation and momentum for their work in rural areas. Priscilla's chapter responded by creating the organizing structure needed to reach into new areas. The low-engagement state also responded by devolving responsibility down into the hands of volunteer leaders spread throughout the state, but those leaders acted as lone wolves. The geographic pressure forced both chapters to realize that they had to spread responsibility out, but one of them adopted an organizing approach while the other continued to employ a lone wolf model.

Interpretation and Meaning-Making through Narrative

Faced with similar resource constraints, why did some chapters choose to organize while others did not? Part of the answer to this question is about the way chapters and the people within them interpret and make meaning out of the challenges they face, their past experiences, and the choices they have before them. For instance, chapters often have stories they tell about past victories and defeats that have implicit causal narratives about why they won or lost. "Remember when we got 100 people to pack the hearing room and they decided to support our cause?" Or, "Remember when Jane wrote that 20-page brief that caused the board to rule in our favor?" Likewise, individuals have their own experiences and their own stories to tell. "I was once part of an organization that used big data really effectively and won the election." Individuals and organizations can also develop narratives by observing the work of other organizations and movements. All of these stories—from individuals, experiences within the association, and observed experience outside the association— contribute to the interpretive frame that organizational leaders draw on when they make strategic choices.

These stories are part of interpretive work that constantly goes on within associations. In writing about the functions of association leadership, Morris and Staggeborg write, "Framing is central to [how leaders strategize] because it identifies both challenging groups and adversaries and suggests potential allies. Framing specifies the unjust conditions that must be changed and the appropriate strategies and tactics to achieve the desired ends."[7] Through framing, or interpretation, leaders develop a shared vision of the challenge they are facing, and what resources (in allies and opponents) they have. These frames influence strategic decisions, even if those strategies are not necessarily the most instrumental options the association has. Over time, James Jasper argues, people (and associations) develop a "taste" for certain kinds of strategic repertoires that are not necessarily related to how useful that strategy may be in a

7. Morris and Staggeborg 2007, 183.

given situation.[8] People also do things a certain way because they believe it is consistent with the kind of people they want to be. Elisabeth Clemens writes, "The answer to 'who are we?' need not be a quality or noun; 'we are people who do these sorts of things in this particular way' can be equally compelling."[9] Interpretations about collective identity, challenges, and strategic options all emerge organically over time through association activity and every day "talk."[10]

In the local chapters I studied, narratives emerged through discussions about where the chapter could draw its power. As sites experienced pressures emanating from leaders without enough time, a geographic turf too large to organize alone, or increasing pressures from a parallel presidential campaign, the leaders had to ask themselves what they could do. They all implicitly asked themselves, "Where do we draw our power?" Drew, a leader in Milton in the National Association of Doctors described his response when he realized that he and the other leaders did not have enough time to focus on the needs of the local chapter.

> Well, so we had to look around and say, "Okay, what can we do? What resources do we have?" We didn't have money to hire someone or stuff like that. What we had was people, and lots of hospitals around and doctors who cared. And that's what the [National Association of Doctors] has always been about for me.

These local chapters had developed interpretive frames that influenced the way they perceived their sources of power. A core belief of the national leaders in the National Association of Doctors was that what set the National Association of Doctors apart from other physician groups was the commitment of their doctors. Thus, when Drew was facing a strategic challenge in his local chapter, his first instinct was to think about that commitment as the key resource he could draw on to meet the challenge.

8. Cited in Polletta and Jasper 2001, 293.

9. Clemens 1997, 50.

10. Polletta and Jasper 2001; Polletta 2006.

Where associations believe their power lies is an important factor in understanding strategic choices. Telling a story that says, "Remember when we got 100 people to pack the hearing room and they decided to support our cause?" is very different from saying, "Remember when Jane wrote that 20-page brief that caused the board to rule in our favor?" The first story implies that the association won because they had more people on their side. The second story implies that the association can achieve its goals if they have the most compelling research brief. Depending on what kinds of stories the association tells, they will think differently about how to conceptualize their problems and mobilize resources.

The multiplicity of possible narratives that exist often makes it hard to see subtle differences, like the ones that exist between mobilizing and organizing. Many leaders of membership-based associations, like Drew, see people as the source of their power. Not all of those leaders, however, see organizing as a solution. When Drew and his colleagues were not able to get the work of the local chapter done, they perceived it to be a leadership problem. Their solution was to recruit and develop volunteer leaders who could take the place of staff. Other organizations could have faced the same problem and interpreted it as a resource constraint: their solution could have been to raise more money to hire staff. Still others could have reached toward a mobilizing solution—perhaps by increasing the size of their list, they can demonstrate their organizational effectiveness to garner more resources for the organization. Drew and his colleagues, however, interpreted the problem as one of a lack of leadership.

The experiences of the leaders affected whether they considered organizing as a solution to their problems. Both Greenville and Fairview, high-engagement chapters in the National Association of Doctors and People for the Environment, respectively, had leaders with previous experience organizing while their low-engagement site counterparts did not. The People for the Environment leader hired a staff member who had been trained as an organizer and pushed the volunteer leaders to adopt organizing as a way of doing things in their state. The National Association of Doctors leader had previously been active in the Civil

Rights movement and had been exposed to organizing in a variety of contexts. When their chapters faced challenges, both leaders turned to organizing as a way of meeting them. The biographical experiences of these individual leaders and the approaches they took illustrate how individual and collective histories influence the ways in which associations interpret their strategic challenges and the choices they make.

In addition, whether they identified organizing as a possible solution to the challenges they faced depended on the narratives they heard from outside the organization. For instance, the media's focus on online organizing in the 2008 campaign to elect Barack Obama, or the viral spread of movements like the Tea Party and Occupy Wall Street in 2009 all feed narratives that association leaders developed about how to build power. Several times, I observed leaders who said something like, "We saw what happened with Obama" or "We saw what happened with Occupy" and "we wanted to try to go viral the same way." After reading stories about the powerful impact of technology in recent campaigns, these leaders developed narratives about the power of online tools as a solution to their problems. Other leaders I observed told different stories. They would say things like, "I feel like there are a few campaigns out there that are really succeeding because they are building depth." They would cite stories about the depth of commitment they saw among volunteers in Obama's 2008 campaign, or the power of conservative organizations like the National Rifle Association to generate deep commitment. Leaders who developed these kinds of narratives were more likely to see the value of investing resources in organizing.

Put together, these individual experiences, biographies, and narratives contribute to a collective identity—or associational culture—that plays a large role in the interpretive work that goes on. This culture interacts with organizational routines, decision-making norms, resource constraints, and other factors to shape the strategic choices an organization makes. The narrative helps associations give meaning to the constraints, opportunities, and changes they see. As new volunteers and new leaders are brought into the association, they hear the stories people tell and learn from the experiences of others. As this process happens repeatedly over time, the people within the association begin to create a shared identity or culture that is passed on from person to person.

Association Structures

Although individual leaders can make the choice about whether to mobilize or organize, their decisions have implications for the entire chapter because each strategic choice affects the structures of responsibility (and culture and narratives) that emerge. In other words, mobilizing and organizing have different implications for how chapters distribute responsibility.

Chapters can centralize control in the hands of paid staff or a few volunteer leaders. Alternatively, they can distribute responsibility through a tiered network of leaders. Tiered networks can be formal or informal structures and be comprised of committees, subcommittees, leadership teams, and other bodies. Distributing responsibility widely makes multiple people responsible for outcomes, but those outcomes cohere into a broader strategy. (An alternate model would be to distribute responsibility around a set of disconnected goals and purposes, such that multiple people have responsibility, but their work does not fit into a coherent strategy.) Organizers tended to adopt what has become known as a "distributed leadership" structure, or a structure that distributes responsibility out to a coordinated network of leaders.

The decisions chapters make about how to distribute responsibility create incentives for whether and how associations go about engaging people in activism. For example, because chapters that distribute responsibility for outcomes widely depend on multiple volunteer leaders to get work done, they often work harder to develop programs to train and support their leaders. The organizers in this study created a structure of engagement that made it impossible for them to achieve their public goals without engaging activists. Mobilizers and lone wolves, in contrast, developed strategies for achieving their public goals that did not depend on cultivating leaders. Thus, any emergence of leaders in their work was a happy byproduct, but it did not affect whether they were able to achieve their goals. By linking leadership development to the pursuit of their advocacy goals, organizers create incentives for themselves to engage in practices that cultivate activism and leadership. When other leaders come into the chapter, the structure in place provides incentives for cultivating activists, making it more likely they will do so as well. Strategic choices about where to locate responsibility, in other words, can condition subsequent choices about how to cultivate activism that make mobilizing or organizing more likely.

Sites that employ lone wolves, like Paul's local People for the Environment chapter, do not make much effort to structure the work of volunteers since each lone wolf is working more or less autonomously on his or her own project. The four key areas in which Paul's chapter worked were (a) forest protection, (b) water pollution, (c) air pollution, and (d) transportation. They chose these areas primarily because there was one person within the chapter with a deep commitment to each of them. Each person working on each of these issues worked more or less alone. Like Paul, most of these leaders had opted for an inside strategy to accomplish their advocacy goals. They focused on administrative hearings, reading and writing research reports, and interfacing with representatives of local administrative agencies. They did not seek to engage the grassroots in activity or influence the administrative agencies through outside pressure, even though, as Paul intimates, they may have wished they could have.

Because each of these leaders worked alone, they did not coordinate strategically with each other. Advocacy in these four areas did not cohere into a broader association strategy. Instead, the leaders set advocacy goals for themselves and then pursued them to the best of their ability. Because they all worked under the name of People for the Environment, they met every few months to update each other on their work and brainstorm ways to support the work. Sometimes they would contemplate building more grassroots power. Yet, they lacked expertise about how to build up a grassroots infrastructure, did not have people who knew how to cultivate leaders, and had, for years, built a culture that relied on inside advocacy strategies rather than grassroots support. They did not have much of a leadership pipeline and, as Paul notes, did not have enough people to "do stuff." People like Paul who were able and willing to take on responsibility took on more and more until some of them burned out. Whenever a leader at one of the nodes would leave, the chapter would struggle to fill the place, and if they could not fill it, simply let work in that area atrophy. Because each of the areas operated independently, one node could wither away without affecting the work of the others.

Leaders in Priscilla's chapter, in contrast, had structured their work through a central leadership team that planned and coordinated all the work of the chapter. A big part of this chapter's advocacy strategy is to educate members about state legislative elections, work to elect candidates who support their cause, and put pressure on those who do not. In between elections, they try to organize "lobby days" at the state capitol, in which they bring as many members as possible to the statehouse to demonstrate the breadth of the chapter and pressure legislators to support their positions. The leadership team, comprised of staff and volunteers, would do much of the planning and coordination around these electoral and advocacy activities. They would develop a strategy for which elections to target, what messaging to use, and how to get people involved. No volunteers outside of the leadership team took any responsibility for this work. Volunteers might participate, but they did not have any responsibility for doing the work. As such, when Priscilla's chapter was still focused on mobilizing, they had lots of volunteers who got involved, but only a very small group of people who took on leadership. The only people who had responsibility or any strategic autonomy were the core staff and leaders.

When Priscilla began incorporating organizing into the work of her chapter, the chapter began to shift responsibility to a wider network of volunteer leaders. Priscilla described this transition as moving from "organizing events" to "organizing organizers." Instead of having all the responsibility for planning events and mobilizing participation in those events, staff and core leaders became responsible for organizing *others*. Core leaders were now responsible for recruiting, developing, and supporting other leaders. Those leaders were responsible, in turn, for organizing events and mobilizing attendance for them. This broadened the reach of Priscilla's chapter and enabled it to develop a broader strategy for accomplishing their advocacy goals.

Figure 3-1 depicts the new distributed leadership structure in which responsibility is spread through the chapter. Instead of having a few leaders who can plan events, there are many leaders with that capability. The core of the chapter consists of the same staff and volunteer leaders as before, but responsibility is pushed to an outer ring of people, as signified by the arrows pointing outward. Because each staff and volunteer leader in the middle takes responsibility for coaching and supporting two or

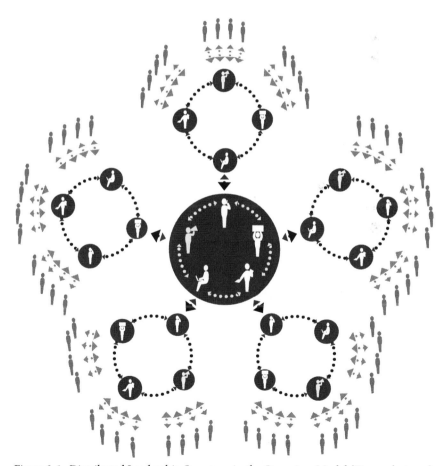

Figure 3-1. Distributed Leadership Structure in the Organizer Model (Figure designed by Jason English, based on leadership models originally designed by Marshall Ganz)

more of the volunteer leaders on the outer ring, the outer ring can have more people in it than the inner ring. Then, each of those leaders on the outer ring acts as an organizer as well, developing a team of people to help plan activity that encourages widespread participation. As a result, the programming activity that the chapter can run and the number of people they can engage in those activities expand. In addition, getting the programming activity done depends on cultivating this outer ring of leaders. Without that layer of leadership, the inner circle of core leaders would be unable to do the programming work.

This structure provides a wider group of people with responsibility and strategic autonomy for doing their work, but coordinates it through a structured coaching system. As a result, it helps the chapter use depth (a core of committed leaders) to achieve breadth (a wider circle of activists engaging in activity). Priscilla describes the transition:

> So we sent out an email blast to recruit a bunch more people to [host events] around the state, to see what happens. We ended up having eleven people sign up to host an event and you know a couple fell through, inevitably. So we ended up with nine events across the state... with some down in places we haven't really done that much organizing. And [part of that] was because what our online organizer was saying: we have good lists. We're pretty active and pretty engaged on our lists and we're making consistent phone calls to people. But, what made nine of these events happen was that I had recruited [a volunteer leader] who just did a really good job of following up and holding people accountable—saying we'll have these weekly calls, these are the materials you'll need, these are what the expectations are, go for it with these events. And we had like 115 people [in one area] where we've like never organized anything. [It's an area] where we were always like we want to do work there. So here we are now.... [The leader who helped build all these events] now has a million things on her plate. We need to really figure out how to keep all of these people engaged.... The next step is to identify some people and ask them to be team leaders and to create their own team in their communities.

Priscilla, recognizing a need to reach new communities to win the campaign, transitioned to supporting a volunteer leader who could support other volunteer leaders who were trying to host events in new areas. By doing so, the chapter was able to expand its work into an area where it previously had not been able to gain any traction. This expansion occurred partly because the chapter had done a good job of building up its prospect list through previous mobilizing activities but also because Priscilla recruited a volunteer leader who could put considerable time into mentoring and supporting new leaders. This leader supported the new volunteers through weekly phone calls, provided them with materials, debriefed them afterwards, and actively cultivated their leadership—activities that Priscilla had never had time to do. Priscilla, in turn, coached the leader in how to develop these new groups of leaders in new communities. Each leader had the autonomy to craft strategy within her local area, but the strategies were coordinated around the state through coaching.

The integration of the advocacy strategy and the organizing strategy created incentives for Priscilla to do her work in new ways. Priscilla's success in the campaign became dependent on her ability to recruit other volunteer leaders who could help support the development of new leaders around the state. She talks about how her goals shifted from "holding events" to "holding one-on-one meetings and doing leadership development." In addition, it created a beneficial cycle. As the chapter became better able to plan programming, its advocacy agenda incorporated a higher level of programming around the state. The only way the chapter could run that programming is by engaging more people as volunteer leaders, and plugging them into the structure. The chapter cannot do its advocacy work, in other words, unless the leaders spend time developing other leaders.

The level of engagement in chapters that did organizing through this kind of distributed leadership structure was consistently higher than in other chapters. No one chapter had a full-fledged organizing model throughout its entire operations. Most chapters had some areas where the organizing model was strong and other areas that used a mobilizing or lone wolf approach. Nonetheless, having even some organizing within the chapter created a structure for activist and leadership development that led to more consistent participation across the chapter.

Organizers distinguish themselves from mobilizers and lone wolves by giving core leaders responsibility for developing other leaders who have responsibility for engaging in programmatic activity that helps the chapter meet its advocacy goals. Lone wolves devolve responsibility down to other volunteer leaders, but those leaders work alone, not opting to involve others in their work. Mobilizers seek to engage widespread participation, but they do so without developing the capacity for others in the chapter to take responsibility for outcomes. Core leaders and staff maintain control. Organizers, by contrast, push responsibility for programmatic activity out to other volunteer leaders, forcing core staff and leaders to focus on developing and supporting those leaders. In doing so, the organizers develop long-term capacity for the chapter.

STRATEGIC "STICKINESS"

Once an association decides to organize or mobilize, certain structures are put in place that contribute to strategic "stickiness" or path dependence over time. Associational cultures, narratives, and structures emerge that influence future strategic choices.

Once leaders make the choice to create a distributed leadership structure, for instance, organizing becomes much easier. Priscilla, for instance, decided to distribute responsibility out to a network of leaders because she could not plan advocacy work for certain areas of the state. Once she had recruited other people, and given them responsibility for planning advocacy work in their area, she had to equip them with the skills they needed to get this work done. Priscilla's strategy and structure, in other words, created incentives for her to act as an organizer and invest time in building the capacity of her volunteers.

Likewise, when associations try organizing, they begin to create narratives explaining their work that contribute to a broader associational understanding about power. Organizers who spend weeks and months building up relationships and recruiting people to attend an event will often create stories after the event explaining its success by the effort they put into it. As will be discussed in chapter 4, creating such narratives and helping volunteer leaders interpret the work they have been doing is a core component of how associations build up leaders. These narratives become part of broader association understandings about power. Where does the association draw its power? When they begin to believe, as Drew did, that it comes from engaging others, then they become more likely to organize again in the future.

A local chapter's strategic choice to organize, mobilize, or adopt some other method of change becomes "sticky" when it is passed on from one generation of leaders to the next. People are not born with the leadership skills needed to run a civic association. Those skills develop through careful cultivation, mentorship, and experience. As new leaders join an association, they learn ways of doing the association's work and achieving the association's goals from existing leaders. In fact, a bi-directional selection process likely exists, in which existing leaders select new leaders who are good fits with the association's strategic culture, while leaders self-select into associations that are good matches for their interests and skills. As this process unfolds, strategic choices an association made earlier get passed on from one set of leaders to the next.

The experiences recounted by Dale, a doctor in the National Association of Doctors, exemplify how having responsibility forces people to learn to organize:

DALE: You know the organization had social functions and at the social functions they would announce what projects were going on and so one day something struck a chord with me and I said, "Oh that is something I could help with, I could devote some time and energy to that."

INT: Right. And had you been involved with the National Association of Doctors for a while in the past?

DALE: No, I just joined so it was within about a year of getting to know them.

INT: Okay. So how did you go from volunteering a little bit of time to getting more involved?

DALE: Very easily. There was [an elected official] that was not very supportive [of our work] and we wanted to get him voted out of office. I mean, our little organization kind of took it under our wing saying, look, he's not supporting our agenda… so we're not going to put up with this. At first I just started coming to phone banks and stuff [for the National Association of Doctors]. Then someone saw that I kept coming so they asked me if I wanted to get involved more by helping to organize and run some of the events. So I thought, "Sure, why not? I can send a few emails to people and show up when I would show up any way and that'll be it." But boy was I wrong. I couldn't just send a few emails and get it to work. So I was like, what do I do? And someone showed me that you have to plan these events, you have to map out your strategy, what are your obstacles, and then take on those little steps one by one. It's not a process that happens overnight, it's something that you have to have a plan and then that plan moves forward. They really had to hold my hand. But then I got it and could do it myself.

When he first got involved, Dale did not know how to organize events or plan actions on behalf of the National Association of Doctors. He got involved because he was interested in the work and thought that he had something to contribute. Once someone asked him to take responsibility for a real outcome—running a phone bank—then he had to start developing new skills. Another leader cultivated those skills in Dale, teaching him how to strategize around his event and overcome obstacles that got in the way of his success. This process of teaching Dale is a good example of organizing. Through his work, Dale became adept at strategizing and planning actions and now has the capacity to do them on his own—and to teach others to do the same. The reason he learned the skills, however, was that he had a responsibility he could not fulfill without them.

Consistently making the choice to invest in developing the leadership of volunteers is no easy task. It takes considerable time and effort, and when associations are faced with the pressure to achieve their advocacy goals, it can often seem easier to delegate work to paid staff members or seasoned leaders who do not need support to get it done. When push comes to shove, even associations with the intention of cultivating the capacity of their volunteers often choose not to do so—unless they have structures and narratives in place that push them to organize. The structures they create to accomplish their strategic objectives creates incentives for the ways in which they will (or will not) engage others in activism.

The narratives they tell about where their power originates also affect the choices they make about whether and how to engage others.

Although investing in organizing can be resource-intensive, it has long-term payoffs for the association. Providing the kind of mentorship Dale describes on a larger scale creates a culture of organizing that persists. Dale was not the only doctor whose skills and capacities improved through the work on the campaign. The lead organizer in this local National Association of Doctors chapter was trying to cultivate a whole network of doctors to become leaders, who could then help plan activity for the National Association of Doctors in their communities. Even when the original campaign Dale got involved in was over, the leadership capacity within his local National Association of Doctors chapter remained. As new volunteers got involved, leaders like Dale could continue to reach out to them, build relationships, and cultivate their activism in the same way his activism was originally developed. This created a beneficial cycle within the chapter.

CONCLUSION

Whether because of geography, the pressures of a presidential campaign, or leaders whose time was getting increasingly tight, many of the high-engagement chapters in the study first began organizing when they faced an external challenge. That challenge prompted chapter leaders to reassess the way they do their work. They drew on organizational narratives and interpretive frames to help them identify the sources of organizational power. When leaders believed that power came from the chapter's membership, they began to make choices to organize. Leaders would begin to redistribute responsibility in such a way that they had to develop other leaders to get the work done. The only way they could meet the demands of their workload was to identify, recruit, and develop other leaders. This work soon became a self-reinforcing cycle, such that new leaders adopted the same practices they observed in more seasoned leaders.

These pressures alone were not enough to guarantee that the chapters would adopt an organizing approach, however. In several instances, low-engagement chapters faced similar pressures but did not respond by organizing. The experience and willingness of the core leaders, the organizational narratives they created, the understandings about power, and the structures that were in place also mattered.

Associations are under tremendous pressure from the media, from funders, and from their members to produce quick results. Often, this pressure can create incentives for associations to ignore the challenging work of investing in their members. Yet this study shows that the best way to get people involved and keep them involved is engage not only in transactional mobilizing but also in transformational organizing. Helping people develop skills and create relationships that have value beyond the specific campaign at hand helps people commit to further activism. Given external pressure, associations were most likely to do this work when they had a strategy and structure in place that created incentives for them to do so.

The subsequent chapters explore the strategies associations used to develop these skills. How did mobilizers and organizers differ in the ways they built their prospect lists and cultivated activism? What did associations actually do to engage more activists?

4

Organizing

David, the Mobilizer

When asked what he does to engage doctors in the National Association of Doctors, David says, "It's really just a lot of turning the crank." In planning activities for his local National Association of Doctors branch, David's key goal is making the work as easy as possible for people. Whether it is contacting an elected official, writing a letter to the editor, or attending an event, he tries to create processes that automate the work for himself and his volunteers. People "don't have to think," he says. Instead, they "just show up, click, or whatever."

Derek, the Organizer

Derek takes a different approach when planning events for his local National Association of Doctors branch. At one point, Derek was responsible for organizing an event in which a prominent local politician was coming to speak to a forum of doctors. In thinking about the event, he asked, "Who do we want to target to fill the room? Do we just want to get 175 bodies who could be anyone, and who just listen and leave? Or do we want 175 people who are going to be the beginning of a network that grows and, if so, then what should that network should look like and what should the event look like?" His preference was to attract people who were willing to take action and use the event to encourage them to think creatively about the actions they could take.

To facilitate interaction among attendees, Derek created a structure for the event that would bring people into contact with people they did not know. First, Derek created an online registration process that asked people to indicate their interests, their background, and what was motivating them to attend the event. Prior to the event, he planned to work with other volunteers to organize this information and group people into different categories using color-coded nametags. When people arrived at the event, they would be given colored nametags and instructed to find someone who had a different color nametag. Attendees could not simply sit back and listen. Instead, they would move outside their comfort zones and talk with someone who had a different background and a different set of interests. Attendees would be instructed to use these conversations to find some shared interest and then discuss things they could jointly do to act on that interest. At the event, Derek would set up a wall where people could write down and post these commitments. People would leave the event, as a result, having developed a new interpersonal relationship with someone in the chapter and a shared commitment to action with that person. The event did not unfold precisely as Derek planned because of concern other leaders expressed about reducing overall attendance at the event if they asked too much of attendees. As a result, the actual event was a hybrid of Derek's ideas and more traditional approaches to such forums.

Instead of looking for "bodies" that just "listen and leave," Derek wanted to use the event as a way to create the "beginning of a network that grows." He designed the event with an eye towards thinking about what kind of experience would be most likely to facilitate further activism among the group of people who attended. David, in contrast, saw his job as making the work as costless as possible for people, so that they would do more of it. David was most interested in getting people to take action, and less focused on the effect the actions themselves could have on people. The contrast between David's and Derek's approaches and the disagreement between Derek and other volunteer leaders about how much to ask of attendees at the event epitomize some of the many tensions civic associations face in engaging members in activity. Should they make participation as quick and easy as possible to minimize the burden for volunteers? Or should they ask volunteers to engage in activity that requires more time and effort but potentially builds greater long-term capacity for activism within the association? Derek hoped to build more relationships with and among activists by asking people to do more than just attend an event.

Underlying Derek and David's divergent approaches to getting people involved are distinct principles that differentiate mobilizing from organizing. As an organizer, Derek was concerned with developing people's capacity to act on behalf of their interests.[1] Developing this capacity is a long process that involves everything from building people's motivation, to equipping them with the skills for action, to creating opportunities and narratives that help them develop the sense that their participation—and collective action in general—matters. The process begins, in many cases, by developing relationships with and among activists. From the outset, Derek was thinking about ways to get people into relationship with each other. David, in contrast, was more focused on maximizing the number of people who took action in the short term by making it as cost-free as possible. Allowing people to work alone required less coordination and made it easier for people, but it did not bring them into contact with others in ways that could transform their motivation for ongoing activity.

This chapter explores the strategies that organizers in the National Association of Doctors and People for the Environment use to engage people in advocacy, develop their capacity for action, and push them up the activist ladder. Examining the different choices low-engagement and high-engagement entities make about how to get people involved reveals distinct philosophies about activist engagement. I begin by describing the underlying theories of transactional versus transformational participation that differentiate assumptions about participation in mobilizing and organizing. Then, I show how the sites focused on mobilizing try to maximize participation by minimizing costs, while organizers try to cultivate activism by transforming people's beliefs about themselves, their work, and the like. Much of the transformational work occurs through

1. See Warren 2001; Smock 2004; Ganz 2009; Speer, Peterson, Zippay, and Christens 2010.

interpersonal, interdependent work, such that activists must work collectively to accomplish their goals. I describe the tactics organizers use to bring people into contact with each other. Once (and as) they develop these relationships, organizers also face the challenge of cultivating activists' skills, motivations, and civic capacities so that they can take on greater leadership roles. I show how organizers provide a wide range of cognitive, technical, emotional, and motivational coaching for activists. Mobilizers, in contrast, often focus only on providing volunteers with technical support. The chapter thus examines the different ways that mobilizers and organizers engage volunteers to reveal their distinct underlying philosophies about participation.

FRAMEWORKS FOR UNDERSTANDING ACTIVIST ENGAGEMENT

Leaders of civic associations make a significant number of strategic choices as they cultivate and support the work of activists. Leaders make choices about the goals and scope of the work, the strategy used to accomplish those goals, and the way the task is communicated to activists. They choose how to define the task, what kind of tasks to assign, and how to pitch the work to volunteers. They have to give activists the direction and the support they need to complete the work and do so in ways that keep the activists coming back. Cultivating activism often involves a significant investment of resources, as it requires leader (or staff) time and effort to provide material, emotional, and technical support. Activists might need technical support to learn how to draft a press release, contact an elected official, or find information about a bureaucratic hearing. Activists need material resources to execute their work, whether it is something as simple as obtaining stamps to send out a mailing, or finding money to host a large event, or acquiring lists of prospective supporters who might attend a house party. Finally, activists often need emotional support, to feel comfortable asking their friends and family to donate to a cause, as well as help dealing with setbacks they may experience in their activism, or support when their motivation to continue engaging in activism flags.

As chapter leaders make choices about how to cultivate volunteers, they can act as mobilizers or organizers. Underlying these choices are distinct assumptions about the purposes and strategies for engaging people in activism. Pastor, Ito, and Rosner distinguish these assumptions by differentiating "transactional" from "transformational" outcomes. They argue that social movements are about "both quantity and quality, both numbers and nuance, both transactions and transformations." One crucial part of movements, they argue, is organizing. "[W]hile you can judge success by the crowds that show up to protest, the more transformative marker is whether leaders grow, develop, and acquire the ability to pivot from issue to issue."[2] Transactional outcomes have to do with things like the numbers of people who partake in a particular action. Transformational outcomes, in contrast, have to do more with the way the act of participation changes individuals, groups, organizations, and constituencies. Leaders focused on transactional outcomes have different approaches to structuring participation than those focused on both transactional and transformational outcomes. The highest-engagement chapters in the study found ways to combine organizing with mobilizing, and achieve both transformational and transactional outcomes.

Understanding these frameworks for thinking about participation can help illustrate the differences in approaches to working with activists. Although mobilizing and organizing are not mutually exclusive strategies, distinguishing the theoretical frameworks that lie beneath each one helps us better understand what they are. The ensuing discussion thus paints a picture of starker differences between mobilizing and organizing than may exist in reality. The frameworks discussed below are not necessarily models the local chapters used to explain their work, but rather lenses we can use to understand the choices they make.

2. Pastor, Ito, and Rosner 2011, 2.

Mobilizing: Transactional Activism

A transactional approach to activism focuses on the quantifiable indicators of the numbers of people who take action—how many people clicked on a link, looked at a page, attended a meeting, made phone calls, or contacted an elected official? Civic associations engage in both mobilizing and organizing to achieve specific advocacy goals, and these transactional outcomes allow them to assess and communicate the extent to which they have a constituency base they can mobilize for action. For associations seeking to build power in policymaking, achieving these transactional targets can be an important source of access and influence.[3]

Because it focuses on achieving transactional goals, mobilizing conceptualizes the relationship between the activist and the civic association as an exchange relationship. Exchange theory says that the relationship between activists and associations is based on exchanging resources that each has to offer the other.[4] Activists have time, money, and effort that associations need. Activists provide the manpower associations need to organize advocacy events supporting their cause, they provide material resources that can support the association, and, in many cases, they provide the sheer numbers associations need to establish their power in the public eye. With more activists, associations can generate more signatures on a petition, more phone calls to a legislator, or more warm bodies at a rally.

In return, associations provide activists with important resources including, first and foremost, opportunities to get involved. Activists who want to do something to support the environmental movement or to address public health issues need opportunities for engagement. Associations provide these and help activists feel like they are contributing to the cause and fulfilling other purposive, solidaristic, or material inclinations they may have.[5] Second, for many activists, associations

---

3. See Hansen 1991 for a description of the way interest groups achieve power by demonstrating that they can accurately provide information about how constituencies will act.

4. Klein, Becker, and Meyer 2009; Blau 1970.

5. Wilson 1973; Miller 2005.

provide an institutional home from which they can engage in their chosen advocacy work. One doctor in the National Association of Doctors, for instance, described the value of having a title when he was doing health advocacy work. Through a blog he had begun, he had gotten very involved in media work around community health issues and enjoyed the fact that becoming an activist in the National Association of Doctors gave him a title he could use when doing that work. Third, associations can provide activists with material resources that may help them achieve their advocacy goals. Because activists have considerable autonomy at the local level, they can help determine how association resources will be directed.

If participation is conceptualized as a transactional exchange between the activist and the association, the act of participating can be thought of as the product of a cost-benefit calculation on the part of the activist. As many scholars of political participation have theorized, people are most likely to engage in political activity when the benefits outweigh the costs.[6] Because political activity is constantly competing with other life demands for attention, people are most likely to engage in activity that they perceive to be a minimal drain on their time and resources. Indeed, a prevalent concern among civic associations is that they will burn out their volunteer activists when the work becomes too costly relative to the perceived benefits.[7]

In this framework, the job of an association leader is to maximize transactional outcomes by creating volunteer work that is as costless as possible. Because time and effort are the most valuable resources activists have, the goal is to make the work quick and easy so that more people will do it. In practice, this means tasks are strictly limited in their time commitment and require minimal effort on the part of the activist. Thus, many associations will assign activists tightly structured tasks. For instance, when asking people to submit letters to the media or policymakers, associations will provide people with scripted templates. They need only to fill in their

6. e.g., Verba, Schlozman, and Brady 1995; Rosenstone and Hansen 1993.

7. Musick and Wilson 2008.

own names and contact information, and perhaps a brief line or two about themselves. This makes it easy for people to submit letters and absolves them of any real responsibility. Instead of having to take the time to compose a letter, they can click a few buttons online, fill in some information, and then submit the letter. These kinds of strategies minimize both the time and effort required by activists and are most useful when the goal is to maximize the sheer number of people who will take action.

When associations are focused on making activism as cost-free as possible for the volunteers, they tend to provide only the technical and material needs activists have. For instance, in order for an activist to be able to organize a house party on behalf of the association, the activist might need some training in how to plan a house party, and a list of members that he or she could contact to invite to the meeting. Support is limited to the information and skills activists need to complete a given task.

Organizing: Transformational Activism

In contrast to transactional outcomes, transformational outcomes focus on the ways that collective action changes the affects, outlooks, and other orientations of individuals and groups. Examples include the increasing ability of people to see beyond their own self-interest, shifts in beliefs about their own agency, or changes in public opinion.[8] Organizers focus on transformational outcomes because these changes make it more likely that people will become leaders within the association, working not only to achieve associational outcomes, but also to recruit others to do so.[9]

In transformational organizing, the goal is not only to get work out of the activist in the short term but also to invest in developing the activist's capacity to act. Investing in this kind of leadership development has several long-term benefits. First, by investing in long-term capacity-building,

---

8. Speer, Peterson, Zippay, and Christens 2010; Christens, Speer, and Peterson 2011; Speer and Christens 2011.

9. Warren 2001; Ganz 2009.

associations make ongoing activism more likely. Second, the work these civic associations do has implications for democracy. Cultivating individual skills and motivations helps to develop civic leaders and the democratic capacities of the activists. In this sense, the civic associations act as true Tocquevillian schools of democracy. Civic associations not only help to advocate for members' interests in the public arena but also help to develop the democratic skills and motivations of their members. Third, these associations develop collective capacity. They help activists realize power by working with others rather than alone. The relational approach goes beyond mobilizing volunteers to organizing and cultivating activists for long-term involvement.

Focusing on transformational outcomes means that the relationship between the civic association and the activist is more than a transactional exchange. In the context of transformational organizing, the choice to take action is not conceptualized as the product of a cost-benefit calculation, but instead is the product of a set of dynamic social interactions. To build the activist's leadership capacity, the association designs activist work that develops collective capacity, instead of furthering isolation. Activists must have opportunities to work with others. People working interdependently are more likely to be committed to their work.[10] When people are working alone, there is a greater burden on the work itself to be intrinsically motivating; if it is not, people lack other sources of motivation. If they tire of the work, or begin to feel like it is useless, then there are no other mechanisms to maintain their commitment. If people are working with others, however, they are motivated not only by their interest in the work but also by their interest in and commitment to the people around them.[11]

A key assumption in transformational organizing is that the interpersonal relationships activists have are the locus of leadership development and transformation. To give meaning to these relationships and contextualize the work activists are doing within the community, associations

10. e.g., Hackman 2002; Van der Vegt and Janssen 2003.

11. Van der Vegt and Janssen 2003.

help activists interpret the work they are doing through reflection. Formalized reflection is a key means by which associations develop long-term motivations and capacities. As Warren writes in his description of leadership development in the Industrial Areas Foundation (IAF), reflection helps people contextualize their work, understand how their actions fit in with the actions of others, and develop their own civic skills. The IAF referred to this kind of leadership development as developing praxis, a "more theoretically informed practice, which, in turn, is consciously reflected upon." He writes,

> In praxis, the most important part of the action is the reflection and evaluation afterward. Our organization plans "actions"—public dramas, where masses of ordinary people collaboratively and collectively move on a particular issue with a particular focus—which sometimes produce a reaction that is unanticipated. This reaction then produces the grist for the real teaching of politics and interpretation—how to appreciate the negotiations, the challenge, the argument, and the political conversation.[12]

Through reflection, activists begin to understand how their work helps develop power for the association. Reflection is crucial for helping leaders understand how their actions fit into the bigger picture, and to develop their skills in navigating the complexities of political action. Reflection also helps leaders understand what they are doing well and what they are doing poorly. It plays a crucial role in coaching, in which coaches lead their mentees through a process of reflection on their actions, to help them identify situations in which they could have done something differently. This kind of feedback is important; only by having knowledge of the results do people begin to develop a sense of agency. They see that their actions have consequences, and they understand that consequences can be both positive and negative. Reflection is the process through which associations help activists see connections between their actions and the results. Finally, reflection helps tie people's work to their individual

---

12. Warren 2001, 221.

identities. Providing support to the activist is not only about achieving a particular objective but also about helping the activist develop an understanding of who he or she is in the context of the work.

Transformational organizing thus differs from transactional mobilizing in the assumptions it makes about why people participate and, as a result, about the kinds of tactics and strategies that are most effective in facilitating further activism. Transactional approaches to mobilizing conceptualize participation as a cost-benefit calculation and seek to create participatory opportunities that are as costless as possible. Transformational approaches to organizing, in contrast, conceptualize participation as the product of dynamic social interactions and seek to create participatory opportunities that maximize the quantity and quality of those interactions.

WHAT DID CHAPTERS ACTUALLY DO?

How are these two different approaches implemented in the work of civic associations? In all the interviews conducted with chapter leaders, I asked them to describe what they did to accomplish their advocacy goals. Because these were open-ended interviews, the answers ranged broadly. Nonetheless, comparing the kinds of activities mentioned by People for the Environment leaders from low- and high-engagement groups provides insight into the ways organizers differ from mobilizers in how they think about engaging volunteers to build power for advocacy. Three main differences emerged. Because organizers were concerned about achieving transformational outcomes, not just transactional outcomes, they were more likely to (a) give volunteers work that brought them into contact with others, (b) provide some strategic autonomy in how the work was done, and (c) structure work into campaign trajectories so that volunteers knew how their piece fit into the whole.

Table 4-1 summarizes the kinds of activities chapter leaders mentioned. The table is divided into three categories. "Activities" refers to general events and actions. "Communications" refers to activities that specifically

Table 4-1. Types of Advocacy Activities Mentioned by Chapter
Leaders in People for the Environment

	Low-Engagement Sites	High-Engagement Sites
Activities		
Trainings	1	1
Research	1	0
Letters to the Editor	1	2
Combined social/political gatherings	0	3
Lobby days	0	1
Celebratory events	0	2
Communications		
Newsletter/mailings	3	1
Online alerts	2	3
Website	2	0
Facebook/Twitter	2	0
Phone banking	0	3
Face-to-face follow-up	0	3
Structure		
Standing committees	2	3
Teams/campaigns	0	2

NOTE: Cells represent the number of sites mentioning each type of activity or action.

have to do with communicating the chapter's message. "Structure" refers to comments interviewees made about how they structure their advocacy work. It is important to note that the table is not a complete accounting of all the work these chapters do; it is an accounting of the things leaders mentioned when I asked about their advocacy work. For instance, none of the high-engagement entities mentioned having a website. All of these chapters do maintain active websites; it simply was not one of the activities that chapter leaders discussed in the context of describing their advocacy work.

The first finding that emerges from table 4-1 is that leaders from high-engagement groups were more likely to do their advocacy work in ways that required activists to work interpersonally with each other. Drew, a volunteer leader with the National Association of Doctors, reflects on the importance of interpersonal work:

> For me, personally, there are two things that drive meaning in my life, and those are people and principles, and both of those two have been areas in which I have found deep fulfillment in the work that [the National Association of Doctors has] done. In terms of the people, I feel like I have found people in our organization, and in our field leadership team, who share similar values, a lot of the values we talked about earlier about the importance of real engagement, the importance of community building, the importance of building a better health care system for all Americans, and the importance of fairness and equity in the care that we deliver. So, there's been a community of shared values that I feel that I've found in [the National Association of Doctors], which has been very gratifying, and has been a big part of what has compelled me to dedicate whatever time I have to the organization.

Drew, like many other volunteers, dedicates time to the chapter because he feels a commitment and a sense of shared value with the other people involved. His commitment is not only to the issues at stake but also to the other people around him. The high-engagement chapters were much more likely to create opportunities for volunteer leaders to work with each other so that they could discover and develop these shared commitments.

Looking at all of the activities and communications work leaders mentioned, it becomes clear that high-engagement entities place more emphasis on work that has a relational dimension. The starkest difference emerges in mentions of combined social and political gatherings. All three high-engagement entities in People for the Environment organize such events, while none of the low-engagement entities do. Combined social-political events include happy hours, dinners, coffees, and bike rides that seek to accomplish an explicitly political goal, but do it in a way that combines socializing with advocacy work. Leaders at high-engagement entities were also more likely to mention lobby days, in which they organize groups of activists to go to the state capitol and lobby legislators, and celebratory events, in which activists working on a project get together to celebrate and debrief at particular benchmark points.

Low-engagement entities were more likely to accomplish their advocacy by focusing on activities that people can do alone. The low-engagement entities organize fewer activities overall, in part because they are unable to generate enough turnout to make social-political gatherings like a happy hour worthwhile. One low-engagement entity mentioned focusing on research. The strategy was to engage volunteers in conducting research on current policy issues and then generating research reports that could be shared with decision-makers. This research, notably, was generally done by one individual with expertise or interest in the area, who worked alone.

Leaders from low-engagement entities were also more likely to talk about their communications strategy as part of their advocacy work. By conflating communications and advocacy, these low-engagement groups revealed an advocacy philosophy that focused more on broadcasting information out than creating advocacy opportunities that brought people in. Even as they communicated information out, they did so in ways that lacked interpersonal contact. When asked how they engage activists in advocacy, leaders of low-engagement groups mentioned that activists could be asked to write for the newsletter, post things on Facebook or Twitter, or maintain the chapter's website. All these activities allow volunteers to work independently on their own schedules. As Penny, a volunteer leader in People for the Environment, puts it, "[The online work] seems to work well because it engages people for a particular instance, a very small piece of time, and once they fulfill that obligation, then we're not asking them to do anything else for a while." Sensitive to the ways in which the work drains activists' time, low-engagement entities structure the work in ways that are as costless as possible.

Leaders of high-engagement entities were less likely to mention communications as part of their advocacy work, but when they did, they were more likely to describe a communications strategy that brought people into close contact with each other. All of the chapters mentioned using online alerts to reach out to and activate their members. High-engagement entities also engaged activists in actively reaching out to other activists through phone banking and as much face-to-face follow-up as possible.

Two of the high-engagement entities mentioned having weekly or monthly phone-banking nights, when activists gather at a central location to call other activists in an effort to engage them in activity. The phone banks themselves are social activities. When I observed one of these events, activists spent the first 15 to 30 minutes socializing over snacks and drinks they had brought to share. Even after they began making phone calls, they would frequently take breaks to chat about conversations they had or things they were thinking about. When one activist finished all of his calls earlier than everyone else, he hung around to support his friends instead of leaving. In addition, the conversations themselves were often quite chatty. While many of the calls they made resulted in leaving a message, when they did reach a person, activists were likely to take a few minutes to chat with the person instead of simply running through a routinized phone script. The activity itself and the way these entities engaged in the activity fostered interpersonal contact, autonomy, and fun.

A second difference that emerged in the way leaders from high- and low-engagement chapters described their work is the extent to which they gave volunteers strategic autonomy to complete the work. Leaders in high-engagement entities reported asking activists not only to attend events but also to help plan them. Planning includes everything from being part of the event committee, to managing logistics for the event, to recruiting others to attend. In engaging activists to plan and attend these events, high-engagement entities gave activists ownership over the work. Patty, a staff member with People for the Environment, noted that attendance at these kinds of events could vary. When asked what explains varying levels of attendance, she replied,

> PATTY: Well, I think one deciding factor is how much time ahead we plan. And the volunteers. So we've had 150 people turn out for talks on the financial assessments for cap and trade. So, it's a pretty dry topic but we get a lot of people engaged when there are a lot of good volunteers involved with it.
> INT: Why do you think having a lot of volunteers matters?
> PATTY: First of all, I think when they're involved at the front end to design something, it's more interesting and compelling to them, so they're

more interested in helping do turnout. And we usually have more time because we've lengthened the planning process to engage them. The content is more interesting and the volunteers are more engaged to help do the turnouts.

Recognizing the importance of giving volunteers ownership over an activity, high-engagement entities give activists decision-making authority over how events are designed and planned. This autonomy affords them greater investment in making the events successful. In contrast, activists in low-engagement entities often have little autonomy in the work they do. Penny says, "An awful lot of what's going on as far as [advocacy] right now is being spear-headed by our staff person. She gives things to activists and tells them what to do so that it's easy for them." Instead of giving activists autonomy in their work, the staff members simplify the work for activists by spelling out directions in as much detail as possible.

A third difference emerged in the way chapters structured advocacy work. Both high- and low-engagement entities mentioned using standing committees. These committees seemed to be of widely varying utility for all of the chapters. They were often issue-based committees whose agendas were relatively undefined and whose work varied based on the energy that people on the committee put into it. Activists could languish on the committee for months or years without any real focus. Two of the high-engagement chapters, however, also mentioned organizing their activists into campaigns or teams that had a defined goal, a clear focus, and were proactive about accomplishing those goals. Peter, a volunteer leader in People for the Environment, describes the difference between committees and campaigns:

> PETER: I think I need to make a distinction between campaigns and committees, and the distinction is that a campaign generally has a beginning and an ending in time, whereas a committee is an ongoing basically never-ending activity…. [W]e have two [advocacy] committees… that are ongoing. They have a little bit of a cyclical feature…. As far as trying to mobilize members in general or across committees for a particular campaign, I don't know of that ever happening.
> INT: Why do you think that is?

PETER: [The committees] are not structured for that sort of thing....
[The committees] have a very long-term.... I don't know what their time-
frame is, probably 50 years. So I think that overall long-term committees, as I think of it, they do have situations which arise which I think
are reactionary; that is, they react to situations which are initiated somewhere else.

Campaign-based teams focused on projects that had a definite beginning
and end, and a clear direction for the work activists were doing. Activists
who were part of campaign teams, in contrast to those on standing committees, had a clear set of goals they were trying to accomplish, and strategies they were using to reach those goals. Campaign teams were better
at providing a sense of meaning about the work because activists had a
better sense of the big picture and the ways in which the work they were
doing fit into it.

In sum, high-engagement entities were more likely than their
low-engagement counterparts to engage activists in activities that
brought them into contact with each other, that afforded them some independence in accomplishing their goals, and that gave them a sense of
the big picture. The use of interpersonal social activities to accomplish advocacy goals, campaign-based teams, and more intensive forms of communication by high-engagement entities seems more likely to motivate
activists to get involved than engaging activists in unfocused standing
committees, isolated communications activities, or research. As such, the
high-engagement entities differentiated themselves from low-engagement
entities not only in terms of what they did but also in terms of how they
did it. In doing so, they revealed distinct philosophies about the way they
build power for their advocacy agenda.

CULTIVATING THE SKILLS AND MOTIVATIONS OF
ACTIVISTS AND DEVELOPING CIVIC LEADERS

Throughout all this advocacy work, how did the organizers cultivate the
capacity of people to lead and take action? How do high-engagement

entities cultivate activists' motivations and skills to develop them as civic leaders? The high-engagement chapters in this study used training and reflection to cultivate activists and leaders. They provided activists with the technical skills they need to do their work and also the emotional and moral support they needed to make the work meaningful. Low-engagement chapters tended to focus more on the technical support, doing less reflective work with prospective activists.

Varieties of Training and Support

Associations can provide both formal and informal support, and activists usually receive both types. Activists receive support informally through the relationships they develop with other activists, leaders, and staff in the chapter. In his study of the Southwest Industrial Areas Foundation (IAF), Mark Warren found that leadership development happens most often through the relationships leaders develop with people they are mentoring.[13] Through their relationships, leaders help new activists develop the motivational and technical skills they need to be active organizers with the IAF. A chapter can also provide support through formal trainings and structured reflection on the work that activists are doing.

A key distinction between mobilizers and organizers is whether efforts focus on the motivational and cognitive dimensions of activist support, or only on the practical issues. Both People for the Environment and the National Association of Doctors use formal and informal mechanisms of support—training, coaching, reflection, and relationship-building—to develop and support activists in their work. High-engagement chapters are distinct from low-engagement chapters in that the support they provide is more likely to acknowledge all three aspects of activism—the practical, emotional, and cognitive dimensions—while low-engagement chapters are more likely to focus primarily on the practical dimensions. In addition, high-engagement chapters are more likely to provide support

13. Warren 2001.

systematically and intentionally. Instead of relying on ad hoc relationships that activists create with chapter leaders and informal coaching that occurs through those relationships, high-engagement chapters offer formal trainings, coaching, and reflection opportunities. These not only help activists acquire the civic skills they need for their work but also help them learn to interpret their work in ways that give it larger meaning. High-engagement chapters thus make greater investments in their activists.

Penelope, a leader in one of the high-engagement chapters in People for the Environment, describes her chapter's approach to training new activists. In her chapter, they start by inviting new activists to a week-long "environmental leadership training program." This training focuses on giving people the technical and motivational capacities they need to become activists.

> [The program covers] the nuts and bolts of how to get butts in seat, how to recruit, how to work with the media, how we talk about [our work] with people… think of outdoor camp where you're canoeing and learning how to tie knots, but instead of that, we're teaching the basics of [political] organizing, and it's a peer-taught, peer-led program, all volunteers.

Importantly, Penelope notes, the program is not just about teaching people a set of skills. It often has the impact of motivating people to become more active in their chapters and communities. She says,

> [T]he folks who come to this program go back and many of them get so involved in [their communities and organizations] that it's a real boon for the [organization] to have the [activists] trained this way…. Oftentimes folks will come to [our training] already being a part of a [a local civic organization]. Sometimes not, but usually that's how they found out about the program. So they're already kind of pre-disposed to at least being interested in environmental work and maybe even activism. Now, a lot of [civic organizations], nation-wide, did what my environmental [group] did—tree plantings, clean-ups. We didn't know what campaigns are. So oftentimes, my role [at the training] is to show people, "Hey, social change is possible on a bigger scale and this is one

model by which you can get there." And it usually just wows the pants
off of everyone in the program. That they are stoked to head back to their
[communities] and implement it there.

The trainings are important for helping people learn skills that they can
use in their activism and also for motivating them to take on more activism. They become motivated when they develop a sense of their own
agency and of the difference they can make. They also become part of
the community of people they meet at the training who share their goals
and values. This helps them develop the personal relationships that can
sustain their motivation, as well as realize that their work is part of something larger. Instead of being an isolated activist, each person is part of
a larger group of people doing similar work throughout a particular locality or region.

In the process that Penelope describes, activists learn the technical and
interpersonal skills they need to engage others in activism, develop the
motivational supports they need to sustain their commitment, and develop a cognitive understanding of the difference their work can make.
As such, the support the civic association provides these activists operates
on all three levels, the practical, emotional, and cognitive. Practical support includes material and technical skills and resources. Emotional and
motivational support helps activists to navigate complex interpersonal
dynamics and maintain their commitment. Cognitive support helps
activists understand why their work matters. As Warren writes, activists
must learn "the art of politics."[14] The art of politics, described this way, is
a complex set of capacities that engages people's practical, emotional, and
cognitive functions.

Piper, a staff organizer in People for the Environment, notes that these
trainings help people make the transition into being organizers, in which
they take responsibility for engaging others in action. She says,

> PIPER: [Before,] our activists used to be representatives. They were very
> much the ones who are speaking at the press conference who are also

14. Warren 2001, 220.

speaking at the town hall, who are the face of the organization.... [Now, we are asking them to be organizers.] And I think this is going to be one of the biggest challenges for our activists who have been around [the organization] for a long time.... It's really hard to just take a step back and say I'm going to take five hours this week and sit down with people and have these conversations with them and find out about their motivations, and passions, and then ask them to commit to this thing. I think, also, it's just challenging for some of the organizers to push people in that way... to push people to step out of your comfort zone to do something that's urgent and necessary. It's not what we're taught—like asking somebody to take 15 hours out of their month to commit to a volunteer position where you're the face of an organization.

INT: Right, okay, so it's hard for people to ask other people to do things.

PIPER: To commit to something. To actually like commit to it and to hold somebody accountable to it. I mean, accountability is, I think, one of the most challenging things that we do as organizers but also one of the most important things.

The transition that Piper describes the activists making in her chapter is very similar to the process that Warren and Ganz describe in their books about organizing.[15] In all of these instances, activists are taking responsibility for engaging others in action. Doing this takes a certain amount of skill, as Piper describes, but also an emotional commitment and courage that many find challenging. In asking other people to make a major volunteer commitment, leaders have to face the possibility of rejection, take the time to have long in-depth conversations to understand the volunteer's motivations, be willing to challenge people to stay accountable to their commitments when their motivation flags, and navigate a number of other complex interpersonal dynamics. Leaders have to be willing to manage a great deal of interpersonal tension, in other words, because they are pushing people to do things they may not do on their own. Managing this tension is central to organizers' pushing people to take on greater levels of activism.

15. Warren 2001; Ganz 2009.

Coaching and Mentorship

As Penelope points out, training does not end with the formal training events. It continues through the mentoring relationship that is created between activists at the training. Sometimes this mentoring happens informally, and sometimes it is formalized through a relationship explicitly designated as coaching or leadership development. Penelope notes that once the training is over, "That's when my role as [a leader] becomes so important… because after [the training], you have this pool of super stoked people who just want to run campaigns and need help doing it." She notes that she would work with her pool of activists by "developing personal relationships" and then "do just some sort of weekly or every other week check-in call." These weekly check-in conversations are crucial for Penelope as she works to help activists develop and implement their skills, as well as sustain their motivation even as the memory of the training itself becomes more distant.

While trainings can begin the process of confronting emotional tension, much of it is processed through one-on-one mentoring relationships. Most often, in both associations, reflective practice happens informally in the relationships activists have with each other. The difference between high- and low-engagement chapters is in the kind of support that these relationships provide. While high-engagement chapters have mentoring relationships that provide practical, emotional, and cognitive support, low-engagement chapters have mentoring relationships that focus primarily on providing technical and structural support to activists.

During the year of the study, I was able to observe a new team being launched in a high-engagement site and a low-engagement site with People for the Environment, and the differences in the way the new teams were supported. In both instances, activist leaders were working with a group of new activists to support them as they launched their team. Each team was responsible for organizing a community around environmental issues related to the work of People for the Environment. Both teams were working in communities in which People for the Environment previously did not have much of a presence, but wanted to develop one because those communities were strategically located.

In the low-engagement site, Patrick, the chair of the state's elected executive committee, identified a pool of potential activists in the new community. He contacted members of the national association who lived in the community, as well as people who had been members in the past but had let their membership lapse. He also asked an individual who had been involved with People for the Environment at the state level and lived in this community to reach out to his personal networks. Through these different approaches, Patrick was able to identify four people who were interested in helping to launch a new committee that would bring the work of People for the Environment to their community. All four had been involved with People for the Environment in the past, but had been less involved in recent years. In addition, all four were civically active in that community, and therefore had a good sense of the social networks, community groups and institutions, and civic dynamics of that area. Finally, because of their experience as civic leaders, they all had a honed set of civic skills they could use to do the work.

Once Patrick identified these people through email, he set up a meeting with them as a group. He traveled to their town and sat down with the group to introduce them to each other and brainstorm things they could do to start the committee. After that initial meeting, he left it to these individuals to run with their ideas. To facilitate their work, he provided them with a list of members in their community they could email and invite to their events and access to an online platform that provided project management tools they could use to organize their work. He also created a group email list so the group could correspond with each other. He put himself on that list so that he could observe their work and step in to answer questions about procedures, policies, and resources available from the state chapter.

Because this team was comprised of experienced civic activists, they were able to launch their committee. Within six months, they had organized three face-to-face meetings, inviting interested community members to join them in organizing environmental awareness activities. Each of these meetings drew 20 to 30 people, and about 15 people signed up to get involved in a subcommittee that would help organize more activities in the area. Patrick provided them with material resources (email lists, access to some funds from the state chapter) and with technical support (online tools for organizing their work, guidance on how to navigate some state bureaucracies), but otherwise let them use their creativity and energy to do the work.

In the high-engagement site, Piper was primarily responsible for launching the new team. She began by identifying a volunteer who had been active in that community but had been working alone for a number of years. She engaged that activist, Paulina, to take responsibility for launching the team in her community. Thus, Piper's role was not to launch the team, but to support and mentor Paulina as she launched the team. Paulina had been an experienced activist and had been quite civically active in her community, but had not formalized much of her work. Piper helped bring greater structure and intention to the work Paulina was doing.

Like Patrick, Paulina began by reaching out to people who lived in the community and had shown interest in the work of People for the Environment. Instead of sending a blast email out to a big list of members, however, Paulina used her knowledge of people who had come to previous People for the Environment events or taken actions online. She reached out to 12 to 15 prospective activists and asked to set up one-on-one meetings. In these meetings, she probed prospective activists about their personal backgrounds to better understand what their motivations were for wanting to get involved. She talked about her own story and her own reasons for getting involved, and then asked each of these people how interested and available they were to take on a leadership role within the community. After these conversations, Paulina consulted with Piper to identify the people she thought would be best to recruit as team leaders. Together, they identified four people they wanted to ask to be team leaders, and Paulina asked each of these people for an explicit commitment of about 8 to 15 hours a month. The four agreed to become part of a team that would work on environmental issues in their community. All of these individuals had done some work with People for the Environment in the past and had been civically active in their community. They had fewer years of experience than the individuals Patrick had identified in his state, but they had compelling personal stories that motivated them to want to take action.

After getting commitments from these four people, Paulina and the four new team members attended a training that Piper organized to teach them the basic skills of political organizing. At this training, the five people were able to get to know each other better, develop a better understanding of their respective motivations, and practice working together through different training exercises. In addition, they were able to spend time developing a basic strategy regarding their early goals and what they wanted to try to accomplish as a team.

Once the training was over, Piper set up a weekly call with Paulina to coach her in leading the team. In each of those calls, they would check-in about the goals they had set the week before to see what they had accomplished, and debrief regarding the work they had done in the previous week. Piper would discuss challenges Paulina might be facing in managing her team, and strategize with her about ways to overcome those challenges. Finally, they would set out goals for the following week. Importantly, this strategizing was not only about the advocacy goals the team had, or the challenges they faced in terms of getting their advocacy done. Much of it was about managing the interpersonal issues on the team, motivating team members to stay accountable to their commitments, and working with Paulina to overcome any personal challenges she may face in pushing her team members. Paulina, in turn, had similar weekly meetings with each of the team members, so that she was providing the same kind of practical, emotional, and cognitive mentoring to those team members.

Weekly calls are essentially opportunities for structured reflection on the work. In these calls, the activists have the opportunity to think cognitively about the meaning of their work and their contributions to it, to discuss emotional challenges they face in getting their work done, and, finally, access resources they might need to complete their work. An example from a call log that Paulina kept of her conversations with her leaders provides a good example of how this reflective process works.

July 27, 2010 | Talk w/Porter, 1:00
Chit-chat: Porter and his sis and Dad went river rafting recently, have their own rafts. Chatted about the trip and how much they enjoyed it.

Outcomes

- City Art event: I asked what direction is this going in now and how can I help?
- How was the meeting w/ City Repair?
  - Porter "It happened." Afterwards Porter says he was thinking of how to make it run smoother. Four total people attended: Porter, Priya, and two other students. Priya wants to work on the project. City Repair might be reluctant to put their name on the project. It's a little more political than what the group usually works on…. Probably individuals who could help though. We talked about how Porter could have made the meeting run smoother, work with Priya ahead of time to make her feel more comfortable, how he could have told his story to get City Repair to sign on.
- Doing some planning. Writing up press release and mural design. We solidified some goals around this.
- I brought up the idea of making a recruitment plan. Especially the people who are on outreach/recruitment team. Talked about pushing them to set some goals, use rules of halves [only half of the people who say they show up will show up].
- Date is set for Monday. Porter talked with [other leaders] about how this event may interact with the board hearing?
- Discussed his fears about the event… the fact that company executives might not be in the city that day… will it make a difference if they are not there? Discussed what the strategy is for exerting our power.
- Last week held a mini-news-conference outside of the company's headquarters in downtown.
  - Talked about what worked well and what to do differently next time.

Next Steps

- This evening he's going to the hearing in the neighboring city.
- Feeling good about preparing your training for the Advanced Training?

- Would it help to think through it together? Maybe next week?
- Objectives?

Paulina began the call with some informal chatting. Although this may seem insignificant, it helps to establish an interpersonal rapport between the two individuals. In addition, Paulina includes notes about the chit-chat in her call log so that she can remember to ask people about it later. This helps give them the sense that she is paying attention to them as whole individuals and checking in on all aspects of their lives, not just their advocacy work. Then they launched into a discussion of the City Art event, in which they were asking local artists to develop art using byproducts from coal produced by the local energy company. This was an attempt to embarrass the energy company by giving the public graphic visual representations of some of the harmful byproducts of dirty energy and generate public outrage about it. Paulina and Porter started by checking in about the goals that Porter had set for himself last week. Paulina knew that Porter had a meeting set up with City Repair to see if they would sign on as a sponsor of the event so she started by asking him about that meeting. As Porter reports, the meeting "happened" but was not as successful as he might have hoped. So Paulina talked him through the meeting, asking him who was there and what he could have done to make the meeting run smoother. They discussed ways that he could have told his own story about why he was motivated to take action as a way of pressuring City Repair, and also the ways in which he could have engaged some of the other people who were at the meeting with him. Thus, she coached him in some of the interpersonal dynamics of pressuring the people at City Repair, and also working with the other activists ahead of time to prepare them for the meeting.

After discussing the City Repair meeting, they then discussed other goals Porter had for helping to plan the art event. They discussed his progress on each of the goals, and Paulina offered some advice regarding areas in which Porter had not made as much progress as he had hoped. She urged him to develop a recruitment plan and gave him some practical pointers about how that recruitment plan should work—in setting target numbers, they should use the "rule of halves," assuming that half of the people who say they will come will not show up.

In addition, Paulina and Porter talked through some of the fears Porter had about the event. This upcoming event was something he was putting a great deal of effort into, and Porter expressed concern that it may not achieve its primary goal of embarrassing the energy company's executives. He was not sure if the event would be successful if the executives were out of town or otherwise did not get the message they wanted to send. Paulina thus used this opportunity to talk to Porter about how and why this event was important, and what implications it had for how People for the Environment was trying to exert its power over the energy company.

They were rushed near the end of the call and were not able to spend as much time laying out the goals and objectives for the coming week. Nonetheless they did discuss a few things that Porter wanted to accomplish in the coming week. Porter was soon to attend an "Advanced Training" for organizers, where he was going to present some of the work he was doing. Paulina asked him if he felt prepared for it, and offered to work with him in the coming week to help prepare.

Through this one-hour call, Paulina was able to offer Porter quite a bit of mentoring on a number of different dimensions. She offered him practical advice about how to set up a recruitment plan for the art event. She kept Porter accountable to the goals that he had set for himself the previous week by asking him about his progress on each of those goals, and thus did quite a bit of work to keep Porter moving forward on his plans for the art event. She offered him practical and emotional advice in helping him understand how he might have better framed the meeting with City Repair, talking about how the interpersonal dynamics worked in the meeting, pushing him to find the courage to use his own story to try to pressure others to take action, and giving him advice about how he could better engage other volunteers in the meeting. She also offered him some emotional support when he discussed his fear of failure around the event, and helped him contextualize the work he was doing so that he could see how it mattered, even if the energy company executives were out of town. In addition, she offered him some practical resources by offering to help him prepare for his upcoming presentation at the Advanced Training.

The weekly calls between Piper and Paulina and Paulina and her team members were thus rich sources of support for the activists. They went much further than providing just the technical advice and resources that Patrick provided to his team leaders. Instead, they built on the initial training that team members attended by consciously reflecting on their practice as these leaders put their organizing skills into practice. Through conscious reflection, leaders were able to hone the practical organizing skills they learned and see how to put them into practice. In addition, they were given access to resources they might not have otherwise found. Third, they were able to make explicit the personal and interpersonal challenges that activists inevitably confront in their work. By making them explicit, they were able to think more intentionally about how to handle them, thereby learning from their practice.

Informal and Formal Reflection

Reflection, such as the weekly coaching calls described above, is an integral part of the work that activists do, because it is the point at which they can step back and learn from their experiences. This learning has both an individual and a collective component. Paige, a veteran activist with People for the Environment, describes the difference between "group reflection" and "private reflection." Group reflection is about helping new activists understand the value of collective action and develop a sense of the power they can build by working with others. In developing new activists, Paige says she starts by engaging relatively novice activists to work with a team of other, more experienced activists to organize an event. Once the event is over,

> a good veteran leader will pull people together after that, to evaluate what we just did. And the person who is relatively new has just experienced

working with others to take some action and now learns about a little bit of theory about what happens when you exercise this kind of power and also [what it means to have] been a productive participant in organizing that.

Experienced activists can help new activists contextualize their work, not only so that these activists understand what role they play in making change happen but also what they are able to accomplish as a group. Through formal reflective meetings at the end of particular actions that the group takes together, they learn from what they did, contextualize it, give it meaning, and then plan for the future. Reflection thus plays an important part in developing activists' sense of collective identity and efficacy, the core building blocks of ongoing commitment to activism.

Private reflection develops the individual activist's sense of personal agency and identity as an activist. Paige says, "[W]hat I love even more is working with someone who is winning because there's that moment where you get to simply say, 'Did you ever think you could do that?'... In that question, it's really a question encouraging her to think about did you ever really think that [you] could do that." She has reflective conversations with her activists to help them develop their own personal identities as activists, to understand the power that they have, and to help them stretch and develop their personal sense of power. She says, "My responsibility as an organizer was to be utterly attentive to the individuals that had decided to become engaged and so very much—I don't like references like care and feeding. I think that's way condescending, but I think it's pretty serious business if you really care about the evolution of something that is important." As an organizer, Paige took a very holistic approach to developing activists. She identified the people who wanted to be engaged and not only provided them with technical skills and support but also was "utterly attentive" to their development as people. She was focused on developing their whole identities, in other words.

Reflective practice works similarly in the National Association of Doctors. Through informal relationships that activists create with each other, they reflect on their experience as leaders. High- and low-engagement sites vary in terms of how much they formalize these reflective relationships. Leaders in the high-engagement sites were more likely to create explicit mentoring relationships with new activists to support them in their work. Although they did not have anything as formalized as the call logs that Paulina kept, they nonetheless had regular check-ins in which the veteran activist would work with the novice to discuss progress on goals, challenges the activist faced, and work together to identify solutions to those challenges.

Dean, for instance, was the core leader who had been running one of the high-engagement chapters. He was transitioning out of his duties because he was becoming more active at the national level within the association. As a result, he wanted to identify other local activists who would be interested in leading the work of the local chapter. The chapter had a major event planned in which the governor was coming to speak with a group of doctors about health reform in the state. Dean used this opportunity to recruit other leaders who could take the reins of the local chapter. He started by identifying promising activists from the pool of people who had been active with the chapter. He assembled a team of about eight people to work together on planning this event with the governor. Each person had a specific role on the team, ranging from outreach, to coordinating volunteers, to publicity, to planning the agenda, etc. Dean set up regular meetings for the team to work together and plan the event. Through the course of this process, he identified two activists who seemed particularly well suited to take on more leadership. They proved themselves to have good instincts around organizing and expressed ongoing motivation to do more.

After the event, Dean had a personal conversation with each of these activists to gauge their interest in getting more involved. They both expressed interest in staying committed so Dean worked with them to plan follow-up from the event. The event with the governor drew many new people to the chapter, and also raised interest in the work of the National Association of Doctors. The activists wanted to capitalize on this opportunity, and Dean stepped back to let them take over. He continued to provide ongoing mentorship to them, strategizing about ways to involve more people, plan events, and revive a previously dormant chapter. The relationship he built with them was much broader than one of purely technical support. Thus, when one of them was considering different career options as a physician, one of the people he went to for professional advice was Dean, because he knew and trusted him.

Dennis, the leader from a low-engagement site, takes a very different approach to supporting new activists in his local chapter. He describes one event in which he was able to recruit eight new activists to come to a meeting about health reform. The goal of the event was to energize the activists to keep them involved in the chapter. He got them there because, "I kept pestering them. I sent many emails around and pestered them basically." Once they were at the event, he describes how he tried to engage them:

> Just—I went through my slide presentation on why doctors should be involved in healthcare reform and basically my larger point is always— and in lectures [and everything]…. That this is our professional obligation. This is our professional duty to support healthcare…. That was the basic message.

When asked if these activists stayed engaged after the meeting, he says,

> Some did…. But, yes, it is hard to say. I don't know that—I mean I know [people] were on the mailing list and I know they got the emails [in which I sent them information they would need] and I know they sent me emails back now and then.

The approach that Dennis took to recruiting and retaining activists was starkly different from Dean's. He made very little effort to get to know these potential activists as individuals and instead focused on providing them with information. He used PowerPoint to impart information in an attempt to motivate action, and then used email to send information about ways to get involved. All of the support he provided, in other words, was purely technical. He never touched on the personal or interpersonal aspects of activism, nor did he know anything about these dimensions of the activists' lives.

I conducted a small experimental study of the effects of reflection to verify its ability to motivate greater activism.[16] This study examined whether engaging in individual reflection with people who had attended an event the National Association of Doctors held with prominent local politicians spurred further activism. In particular, I wanted to see whether engaging in reflection made it more likely people would attend a follow-up meeting. Everyone in the study received a call inviting them to attend the follow-up meeting. Only a subset of randomly selected people, however, were also asked to reflect on their experience at the first event, asking what they liked and did not like, and what else they thought they could do have voice in the political process. Results from the study showed that people asked to reflect on their experience were much more likely to attend the follow-up meeting. Asking people to reflect on their experience and to contextualize the meaning of their participation had a powerful effect in this study on whether people attended a follow-up meeting.

This experimental study of reflection is much more tactical and less intensive than the kind of reflection that organizers who are trying to develop leaders engage in. As discussed above, much of that reflection occurs in the context of a long-term relationship in which the organizer has weekly phone calls with an activist, or some other kind of ongoing relationship within which the activist is coached and developed as an activist. In this study, people were called by a stranger and asked to think about their participation in a relatively large event (in which the power of any one person's role is diminished by sheer numbers). Nonetheless, having a conversation with people about their participation in the event did seem to make it more likely that they would continue to stay involved with the National Association of Doctors. This finding implies that the longer term, more intensive reflective practice has the potential to be a powerful organizing tool.

16. See Han 2014 for details on the study.

CONCLUSION

This chapter described the divergent approaches mobilizers and organizers took to engaging and supporting volunteers in advocacy work. The differences in the choices mobilizers and organizers made in terms of what kind of work to give to volunteers, how much autonomy to give them, how to structure the work, and, finally, how to support the work revealed differences in their philosophies of engagement. The low-engagement sites in the study focused primarily on mobilizing, were more interested in giving volunteers work that was as costless as possible, and did not challenge their emotional or cognitive capacities. The high-engagement sites, in contrast, acted more like organizers, creating interdependent work for volunteers that gave them some strategic autonomy, was integrated into larger campaigns, and was supported through significant training and coaching.

Distinct philosophies about transactional mobilizing and transformational organizing underlie these choices about how to engage with volunteers. In transactional mobilizing, the chapters were most focused on minimizing costs to maximize the numbers of people involved. In transformational organizing, the chapters were focused on creating experiences for volunteers that would begin to transform their affects and orientations towards activism. Thus, they were more likely to create work that brought people into contact with each other, and support that work through extensive coaching. Low-engagement entities were much more likely to engage activists in advocacy work that did not require any interpersonal interactions with other activists. In addition, they were less likely to use trainings or reflection to provide activists with a sense of meaning about their work. When they were successful at running events or building new teams, they often relied on activists who had built their skills and motivations elsewhere and were applying them within the context of the People for the Environment or the National Association of Doctors. The low-engagement entities themselves did not make any effort to further cultivate those skills and motivations. As such, they were behaving more like mobilizers.

To engage activists and build power, civic associations need to act as both mobilizers and organizers. They need to mobilize large numbers of people for short-term activity, showing their power to mobilize the citizenry on important issues. In addition, their mobilization work also helps them to develop pools of potential activists. By identifying people in the population who are sympathetic to the cause, the mobilizers lay the groundwork for the organizers. As organizers, the associations then take those prospects and cultivate a subset of them as activists and leaders. These leaders can they lay the groundwork for future mobilization at scale. By cultivating the motivations and skills that will transform people into more deeply engaged activists and civic leaders, organizers make it possible for associations to develop breadth.

5

Mobilizing

A central tension in organizing exists between doing the deep transformational work described in the previous chapter and doing it at scale. In other words, how can associations reach their transactional goals even as they engage in transformational organizing? To resolve this tension, the high-engagement entities in this study blended organizing with mobilizing. Transactional mobilizing strategies helped them build longer lists of activists at each rung of the activist ladder, and reach more people more quickly than they could with organizing alone. These lists became prospect pools from which they could draw for transformational organizing.

As associations develop and deploy transactional mobilizing strategies, they can do so in ways that lay the foundation for future transformational work or not. Low-engagement entities in this study were more likely to focus solely on mobilizing without an eye towards the way mobilizing could lay the foundation for organizing. High-engagement entities mobilized in a way that helped them lay the foundation for future organizing. Mobilizing and organizing had downstream effects on each other that together, helped these chapters achieve scale. This chapter describes the transactional mobilizing strategies associations use and the differences in how low- and high-engagement entities reached their transactional goals.

Modern civic associations face the temptation to focus exclusively on mobilizing because of the ease with which mobilizing can now be done. Online technologies, the dawn of big data, and other changes to the information economy enable modern-day civic associations to mobilize a broader base more easily than before. For instance, to build their lists, associations previously relied on door-knocking, phone calls, or print media advertisements. The Internet and micro-targeting processes now allow associations to reach a much bigger swath of the population much more efficiently and cheaply. Once prospects have been identified, the Internet allows associations to offer them an array of opportunities for participation. Associations can thus build bigger lists more quickly, and constantly engage in a search process for new activists. The ease with which associations can achieve these transactional goals can make it seem like the tedious work of transformational organizing is not necessary. In this study, however, the highest engagement entities were able to maintain their levels of engagement over time because of the way they coupled mobilizing with organizing.

This chapter describes how civic associations operating in this contemporary environment get to scale by integrating transactional mobilizing with transformational organizing. Drawing on observational data from the comparative case studies, I show that all of the sites, whether they are low-engagement or high-engagement, organizers or mobilizers, working online or offline, engage in mobilizing. One way to characterize this mobilizing is as an ongoing search process through which associations seek to identify groups of people who are most likely to take action. The goal of these activities is to recruit new people to affiliate with the association, and to activate those who may not have taken action. Associations can use a range of different transactional strategies to conduct this search. High-engagement entities distinguished themselves by using mobilizing strategies that had other beneficial, "downstream" effects for the association—such as building the leadership capacity of those who were doing the mobilizing or laying a relational base with those who were being mobilized. These downstream effects helped create a cyclical relationship between mobilizing and organizing: mobilizing built the prospect pools organizers needed to develop leaders. The leaders developed through organizing then became part of distributed leadership structures that expanded the capacity of the association to mobilize others. With more organizers doing mobilizing, the highest-engagement entities in the study achieved scale. In this chapter, I describe the kinds of methods chapters use to mobilize and also discuss experimental research showing how mobilizing strategies with downstream relational benefits can be more effective than non-relational strategies.

DOWNSTREAM EFFECTS OF MOBILIZING AT SCALE

Expanding their pool of activists by recruiting more people to join and take action on behalf of their cause is an important source—and signal—of power for membership-based associations. By demonstrating that they have a large and loyal membership base, civic associations are more likely to gain access to policymakers, have a seat at the table in policy debates, and be part of coalitions fighting for change.[1] Associations thus expend many resources to get more names on a petition, more people to a rally, or more phone calls to an elected official. Measuring these transactional outcomes is an important way for the association to track and demonstrate its power.

As associations engage in mobilizing, they can use strategies that have beneficial downstream effects for the association or those that do not. "Downstream" effects refer to ancillary effects that a mobilization strategy can have on the association above and beyond the instrumental goal of mobilizing people for activity. In her analysis of the role of digital media in contemporary social movements, Tufecki calls these downstream effects "network internalities."[2] These downstream effects, or network internalities, can include everything from increasing the leadership capabilities of those doing the mobilizing, to creating greater social capital within the association, to the development of structures within the association to facilitate communication and coordination of work. For associations like People for the Environment and the National Association of Doctors, downstream effects that enhance the association's capacity

1. Hansen 1991; Baumgartner, Berry, Hojnacki, Kimball, and Leech 2009.

2. Tufecki 2014.

for collective action are particularly important. A classic example of mobilizing that ignores downstream effects is a political campaign that runs get-out-the-vote (GOTV) phone banks or door-to-door canvasses without any regard for the experience of the volunteers making the phone calls or going door-to-door. A campaign focused only on the transactional outcomes would treat those volunteers as interchangeable workers whose sole purpose is making more calls or knocking on more doors. A campaign concerned about the downstream effects of GOTV mobilization efforts could structure the phone bank or a canvass in such a way that it built the skills and motivations of the volunteers conducting the phone bank or canvass. The association could do this by adhering to some of the principles of transformational organizing described in the previous chapter—allowing the volunteers some strategic autonomy in how they conducted the phone bank, structuring it in ways to maximize authentic interpersonal interactions, or making it clear how the outcomes from this phone bank fit into the larger campaign strategy. The downstream effects, or network internalities, of the phone bank then become the increased leadership capabilities of those running the phone bank.

An unexpected byproduct of digital mobilizing is the lack of certain downstream effects that used to emerge from the work of everyday movement-building. In examining twenty-first century uprisings like Occupy Wall Street in the United States, Tahrir Square in Egypt, and Gezi Park in Turkey, Tufecki argues that the rise of digital mobilizing lowered the "coordination costs" of building the uprisings but "may have the seemingly paradoxical effect of contributing to political weakness in the latter stages, by allowing movements to grow without building needed structures and strengths, including capacities for negotiation, representation, and mobilization."[3] Because these uprisings never had to create structures for leadership, they were challenged when it came time to negotiate for policy gains. This gap, Tufecki argues, can partly explain why these uprisings seemed to "fizzle out" or achieve fewer "policy or electoral outcomes" relative to their "size, energy, and scope." Whereas the work of bringing large groups of people together to occupy a public space used to

3. Tufecki 2014.

force associations to create structures for coordination, communication, and, inevitably, leadership, the digital mobilizing that formed the basis of these twenty-first century movements did not. They were able to achieve their transactional goals—getting large numbers of people to occupy a public space—but the process of achieving them did not have the same downstream effects.

The highest-engagement entities in this study, in contrast, integrated mobilizing with organizing to achieve their goals. By organizing, they were able to develop the leadership capacity they needed to mobilize at scale. Many of these entities sought to develop a distributed leadership structure (similar to the one described in chapter 3) with ever-expanding networks of leaders capable of mobilizing others. With more leaders developed through transformational organizing processes, there would be more people who could do the mobilizing—thus enabling the entity to get to scale. Organizing, in this way, fueled the mobilizing. Likewise, by mobilizing, these entities were able to develop larger prospect pools from which they could draw more leaders to organize. By mobilizing with downstream effects in mind, associations could create prospect pools that were better primed for collective action. Paying attention to the two-way relationship between mobilizing and organizing, in other words, enabled these entities to achieve the scale they desired.

STRATEGIES FOR LIST-BUILDING

What are the different kinds of downstream effects that can emerge from mobilizing? Examining the strategies the associations used to develop their pool of prospective activists at each rung of the activist ladder uncovers some of these downstream effects. Recruiting activists involves the dual challenge of identifying people who might want to act and activating them to take some action. To meet this challenge, associations constantly reach out to as many people as possible. They may refer to this process as "list-building," "recruitment," or "building a prospect pool," and the goal is to identify—and motivate—those in the broader population who are potentially interested in their cause, candidate, or effort. People for the

Table 5-1. Mobilization Strategies Used by the National Association of Doctors and People for the Environment for Building a Prospect Pool

Level 1 (Marketing)

Website

Facebook/Twitter

Tabling

Newsletters/mailings

Visibility

Buying lists/membership drives

Level 2 (Individual Outreach)

Phone banks

Canvassing

Friend to friend outreach

Level 3 (Functional Outreach)

Policy education, such as webcasts, teleconferences, speakers, panels

Online action alerts, such as petitions, requests to contact elected officials

Online social expression, such as sharing stories via surveys or social media

Requests to donate money

House meetings

Recreational events: film festivals, happy hours, etc.

Town hall meetings

Environment and the National Association of Doctors both use a broad range of strategies to build the pool of potential activists by activating inactive members and identifying new people who are sympathetic to their cause. Many of the strategies the associations used to mobilize are listed in table 5-1, where they are organized by the extent to which the approach has downstream effects for collective action within the association. The forms of recruitment least likely to have downstream effects for collective action are listed in the top group, and those with more potential for downstream benefits are in the bottom group. These groupings are relatively loose groupings, as almost all of these activities can be done in such a way that they could have downstream effects on collective action. The groupings here are based on the ways they were commonly used in People for the Environment and the National Association of Doctors.

Level 1 Strategies: Marketing

The strategies in the first set in table 5-1 are primarily marketing strategies that (given the way they were conducted in People for the Environment and the National Association of Doctors) had few, if any, downstream effects on the association. I call them marketing strategies because they are primarily about each chapter making information about itself available to potential supporters, hoping that sympathetic people will come to them. These strategies include things like building an organizational website, hosting a Facebook page, and tabling at public events. In all of these situations, the chapter is hoping that its reputation, word-of-mouth, or other marketing strategies will drive people to their table or website. Once people get there, the chapter's job is to make the work seem as appealing as possible so that people will sign up. They send friendly volunteers to fairs, festivals, and other public arenas to try to generate more names. Many of these chapters expend quite a bit of time and energy on building an attractive website and Facebook page, so that people who visit those sites would volunteer.

The philosophy behind these strategies is, in a sense, "if we build it, they will come." Chapters relying on these strategies design the most appealing event or website they can, hoping that once people find it, they will be persuaded to participate. Some chapters devoted much time to designing a sophisticated website, thinking that if they make their web presence more appealing, people will be more likely to sign up to volunteer. When asked how they recruit people to attend events, for instance, one volunteer leader in People for the Environment said,

> Well, we post them on a website or send out postcards. So, if you go to [our] website, you can find any of the events that have been posted by the group. And there's a little pop-up window that comes up that tells you more about each event. There's a calendar for each month…. And it's color-coded by each group. And then you just click on the event that you're interested in and it gives you more information, all the contact information, who to call and how to sign up for it, etc. So I think a lot of people can access the events information that way.

Some chapters used these websites as their primary recruitment tool. They worked to make the website as clear and user-friendly as possible, making it a useful purveyor of information for potential activists. The websites did not, however, provide people with the motivation to go to the website or actually take action. Because these strategies rely on the overall brand name and reputation of the chapter to generate traffic, they are the most passive way of searching for prospective activists.

The downstream effects of these marketing strategies are limited to the association's ability to mobilize information or technical expertise. The chapter might have to find someone who knows how to build a website, figure out ways to present information at a tabling event, or find a vendor who could conduct a membership drive for them. Within both People for the Environment and the National Association of Doctors, this was the kind of work that was often done in isolated silos, such that people's capacity for collective action did not change. Instead, the association focused on meeting its transactional goals—building a website, having people at a tabling event, buying a membership list—without regard for how it might have other beneficial effects for the association.

Underlying this and many other approaches to mobilizing is an assumption that mobilizing is primarily about activating people's latent interests instead of transforming their interests.[4] Schier defines activation as a "finely targeted, exclusive" approach to getting people involved in which "[c]andidates, interests, and consultants carefully identify those in the public most likely to become active and then employ a variety of inducements to stimulate the action."[5] Hutchings also describes activation.[6] He argues that there are large groups of people who have latent interest in particular political and policy issues. For the most part, these people are quiescent, as long as elected officials and policymakers are not doing anything that threatens their interests. As their interests begin to be threatened or opportunities to act on their interests arise, these people

4. Hutchings 2003; Skocpol 2003; Schier 2000.

5. Schier 2000, 3, 8.

6. Hutchings 2003.

become activated through the media and advocacy organizations and can rise up and perhaps sanction their elected officials. Hutchings calls these groups of people "sleeping giants" because they can often seem disinterested in politics or policy issues as long as they do not perceive any threat to their interests. To activate their interest, civic associations must provide them with a stream of information about changes to policy and politics and opportunities for people to get involved. The focus is not on transformation, but instead on activating latent interests. People may or may not have a latent interest in a given issue and associations are not trying to do anything to affect that. Instead, they want to reach out to people who they know are sympathizers and activate their interests so that these previously quiescent sleeping giants will rise up and take action.

In this regard, mobilizing can be conceptualized as a process of continually narrowing people into an increasingly refined group of self-identified supporters. In their description of the Dutch peace movement of the 1980s, Klandermans and Oegema distinguish between "consensus mobilization," in which the association seeks to build consensus for their cause in the general population, and "action mobilization," in which associations figure out who will take action. [7] Consensus mobilization is about separating those who express a willingness to affiliate with the association from those who do not. Action mobilization is about differentiating those who want to take further action with the association from those who do not and figuring out how much action those people want to take (in other words, where they want to place themselves on the activist ladder). Action mobilization works by targeting people for different types of action, asking people to take those actions, and, finally, seeing who takes action. In their case study, they found that three-fourths of the general population sympathized with the cause, and three-fourths of those people had been asked to take action. Among those asked to take action, one-sixth expressed interest in taking action, but only one-third of those actually took action in the end. The pool of prospective activists progressively narrows as mobilization processes segment those who will

7. Klandermans and Oegema 1987.

actually engage in activism from those who will not (and those who are not interested in any activism at all).

Level 2 Strategies: Individual Outreach

The second set of strategies involves reaching out to individuals through activities specifically designed for list-building. These include organizing phone banks, canvassing, and asking existing members and supporters to reach out to their friends. Although some associations hire professional list-building firms to do phone banks and/or canvassing to help them build their list and identify new supporters, none of the entities in this study did. Activities may include door-to-door canvassing in neighborhoods likely to have residents predisposed to the chapter's cause, or hiring canvassers to stand in public spaces and stop people who may show interest in the chapter's work. Other local chapters organized weekly phone banks in which volunteers would call through lists of people to see if they were willing to support the chapter's work. Regardless of the mode of outreach (i.e., door to door canvassing or phone banks), the goal was to engage volunteers in the task of lengthening the list of people the chapter knew were sympathetic to the cause.

These strategies are differentiated from those in Level 1 because chapters set them up to have downstream effects on the volunteers engaged in phone banking, canvassing, or reaching out to others. Unlike passive marketing strategies, these strategies involve intentional outreach to others. In reaching out, chapters did not do much to try to persuade those who were not already interested and instead tried to identify those who were already sympathetic and ready to take action (whether it was joining the chapter, or taking some other action with the group). Even though the interaction with the target was transactional, the effects on the volunteer could be transformational. For instance, previous research shows that once people commit publicly to a position, they are more likely to remain committed to it.[8] Once people declare their support for the association

8. Cialdini 2001; Cialdini and Goldstein 2004.

to others, they are more likely to remain supportive. Chapters can thus use individual outreach strategies to build their lists of potential activists and simultaneously reinforce commitment among their existing activists. One field leader in the National Association of Doctors said that he used to ignore the association's requests to reach out and recruit others. Once he started activating others, however, he became more committed:

> [My job as a field organizer] is mainly trying to recruit people and have small events at bars, not really people's houses, but small events to discuss letter writing, op-ed writing, and more recruitment. So it's definitely about identifying those people who are already pretty interested…. [When I first started, National Association of Doctors] provided a list of people who'd just signed up on the volunteer website and I got their phone numbers, I get their email addresses. I would email out to this group of 50–60 people. Then I would identify medical students in my med school…other residents as well, my own friends, throw them on there, probably email on the order of 100s or something like that. [Once I emailed that whole list, I] maybe got it down to a group…maybe on the order of dozens of people who would actually email back. And among those, probably a core group of less than 10 people [who would show up]. We would get together and then we would say okay, you know we should get together and talk, we should just meet each other and just get something going. And we did. And I found myself wanting to do more.

Once this leader was recruited for and accepted a titled leadership position within the National Association of Doctors, he had to start reaching out to others. Even though he was reaching out to people via transactional emails, the process of doing so built his commitment and his leadership capacity. He explicitly notes that his goal in sending out these initial emails was to identify and activate those who are already interested in activism. The downstream effect was on himself, as he became more committed to the chapter.

Level 3 Strategies: Functional Outreach

The third set of strategies in table 5-1 involves integrating list-building into other advocacy work the chapter might do. In his analysis of mobilization

in contemporary civic associations, Peter Murray argues for the importance of "functional mobilization," or mobilization strategies that engage
not only people's issue-based, purposive motivations but also those that
provide benefits and services that cater to people's everyday needs—such
as the National Rifle Association providing accident insurance, or unions
negotiating for better wages for their workers.[9] In associations doing
functional mobilization, people may join not because they care about the
political issues at stake, but because they want access to certain benefits
or services. This third set of strategies, which I am calling "functional
outreach" refer to mobilization strategies that serve multiple purposes for
the association and, correspondingly, often speak to multiple motivations
a person might have for taking action. Functional outreach strategies can
include everything from hosting speakers to educate the public about an
issue to sending online action alerts for people to get involved. Unlike
Murray's account of functional mobilization, the functional outreach
strategies I describe do not provide direct benefits or services to members.
An important downstream benefit, however, is that they allow the association to fulfill its advocacy functions simultaneously with its recruitment
functions. In many cases, functional outreach also provides people with
opportunities to work on issues they care about in the context of social
relationships they desire. Functional outreach strategies thus have multiple downstream effects on the association.

Chapters often structured functional outreach activities not only to
get people involved but also to build social connections with people.
Mobilizing can be done in ways that do or do not emphasize the interpersonal, relational connections between members of the association and
between the association and its members. Emphasizing relational connections increases the probability of action because it builds on people's
solidary motivations as well as their purposive ones.[10] Many functional
outreach strategies engaged social and purposive motivations to draw in
more people. For example, many of the local People for the Environment

9. Murray 2013.

10. Wilson 1973.

chapters hosted monthly meetings that anyone could attend. They would bring in local speakers or show films in an effort to build attendance and encourage further activism. One leader thought of the monthly meetings as "geared towards trying to get people in that haven't come in before." Another leader says that these meetings are about trying to get people "energized." These functional outreach strategies lay the foundation for future organizing by enhancing the social commitments people may have to the association. By engaging people's social motivations, the association sought to enhance the downstream effects not only on the people doing the recruiting (as in Level 2) but also on the people being recruited.

At all of these events and activities, chapters have sign-in sheets and place existing activists in prominent places to provide new people with information about the association. The National Association of Doctors frequently gave their seasoned activists and leaders buttons to wear that said, "Ask me about the National Association of Doctors." Both associations, but particularly the National Association of Doctors, often asked people to sign-up for events online before attending, so that they would be sure to get people's contact information. Some events actually took place online, such as online webinars with prominent speakers. New and existing members may be attracted to the webinar because of the speaker and, in signing up for the event, provide their contact information to the chapter to use for future activation.

The intensive nature of this third set of online and offline strategies meant that the downstream effects were not just about increasing people's motivations but also their coordination and planning skills. Volunteer leaders had to plan programmatic activity that would attract new people to the chapter. They had to identify speakers, find venues, organize webinars, or pull together resources to host an event. They had to organize surveys, petition drives, or other activity online. All of these activities helped build the leadership skills and structures that the association could later draw on for other purposes.

Even when recruiting people at higher levels of the activist ladder, these outreach strategies involved a transactional exchange. One leader in People for the Environment describes a strategy of recruiting leaders from other organizations:

> Well, we've been trying to find people who have been active already and work with them, sort of synergize. It's not necessarily been the case that we've tried to co-opt them into [People for the Environment], but that's happened sometimes…. Some of the people that were at the meeting the other night that you attended had had campaigns that they'd been going on, and they've either needed some funding or some volunteers to help out, and we suggested that you can work with us on those. Indeed, the people who have headed those initiatives have subsequently come on board as members of our [leadership team]. [We chose these people because] we knew that they weren't just idea people. They were people who actually did things. They organized letter-to-the-editor writing campaigns and workshops, they organized media sessions, they organized rallies and phone banking systems, and they were really doing stuff…. We wanted people who were actually hands-on, get out and do stuff. And that's how we selected them.

The recruitment strategy this leader describes focuses explicitly on finding people who have a demonstrated record of activism, who are already motivated to take action, and who have the leadership skills needed in core activists. Instead of transforming leadership capacities, in other words, the chapter seeks to find people who already have those capacities and bring them on board. When approached to get involved with People for the Environment, these activists are often willing because they recognize the mutually beneficial resources that an alliance could bring.

> I think in part because they saw that we had been doing stuff and that we had a membership that, perhaps, could be mobilized even more, and that we had some resources and we have some money that we can pay when you want to make flyers or brochures, or buy film rights, that, hey, we can do it…. But they weren't just looking for extra resources. They wanted to make things happen.

This strategy was a more aggressive form of recruitment than the others, but it was often successful because it started with a very likely pool of potential leaders. Bringing these people and their resources into the organization benefited the leaders involved, but also had other down-stream effects for the association.

As associations build the pool of prospective activists at all rungs of the activist ladder, they can mobilize people in ways that have no down-stream effects on the association's capacity for collective action (Level 1), effects on just those doing the mobilizing (Level 2), or multiple effects on people and the association (Level 3). The constant requests for action and involvement that characterize the mobilization process constitute an identification process in which the association builds and refines the list of potential activists at each level of the activist ladder to achieve its transactional goals. Associations engaged in functional outreach sought to affect not only the people doing the mobilizing but also those being mobilized. One way the association could enhance the downstream effects on people being mobilized was to create a relational basis for future action. While some associations take a passive marketing approach to recruiting people for activity, others take a more interactive approach that emphasizes the interpersonal, social aspects of participation. The extent to which associations use relational mobilization tactics was among the key factors that differentiated high-engagement locals from low-engagement locals.

HOW DO THE MOBILIZERS DIFFER FROM THE ORGANIZERS?

All of the chapters in the study engaged in at least some of the activities described above to build their prospect pool, whether they had a history of low or high levels of activism. What differentiated the high-engagement organizers from the lower engagement mobilizers was the fact that the chapters focused on organizing were more proactive in building their lists and more likely to use mobilization strategies that had downstream effects on the association's capacity for collective action. Often, this meant using relational tactics that appealed simultaneously to people's purposive and solidary motivations. Even in engaging in transactional mobilizing, the high-engagement chapters, in other words, were more likely to engage in functional outreach to lay the foundation for future transformative work.

The relationship between mobilizing, organizing, and scale becomes clear in looking at the way high and low-engagement sites differed from each other in developing leadership for mobilizing. High-engagement chapters could be more proactive in their list-building work because they often had leaders who were responsible for recruitment. These leaders had usually been recruited and developed through a transformational organizing process. Because the high-engagement chapters engaged in organizing, they had more leaders who had the capacity to help them better mobilize. All three of the high-engagement sites studied in People for the Environment, for instance, had a membership or recruitment coordinator. This person would interact with other leaders to ensure that they were taking advantage of the list-building opportunities at their events. If another leader planned a house party or a movie night, the recruitment coordinator would make sure that sign-up sheets, information about the local chapter, and other materials needed for recruitment were available at the event. Among the low-engagement sites, only one had a recruitment coordinator. In the National Association of Doctors, all three of the leaders in the high-engagement sites viewed list-building and mobilization as a central part of their responsibilities. In the low-engagement sites, leaders were more likely to disavow this responsibility. For example, when asked about the strategies he uses to engage people in activity, a National Association of Doctors leader (in a low-engagement site) said "I don't think anything about that—anything outside of what [the national organization] was doing for us." These leaders did not see mobilization as part of their responsibilities. Without anyone responsible for recruitment or list-building, the task often fell through the cracks, and the chapter was left with only the most passive recruitment strategies.

High-engagement chapters were also more likely to use more of the strategies with beneficial downstream effects listed in the second and third tiers of table 5-1. While all of the chapters studied had a website, for instance, only high-engagement chapters reported doing phone banking to reach out to potential supporters. Most of the chapters reported hosting local events (such as speakers, talks, social events, etc.), but the high-engagement chapters were much more likely to use these events to recruit people. When asked whether they recruit people through any of their monthly meetings, for example, one leader from a low-engagement group in People for the Environment said, "Yes, well, they come. But I don't know if we have lists of who they are or what happens to any sign-up sheets." The high-engagement chapters, in contrast, recognized the importance of face-to-face activity and actively tried to use any kind of local event as an opportunity to recruit more people to the chapter.

Low-engagement sites struggled to do anything more than the most passive mobilizing because they lacked leadership resources. Instead of just creating a website and a Facebook page, high-engagement chapters would actively direct traffic to the sites by constantly announcing it at events, working with partner organizations to direct traffic to the website, and utilizing other advertising opportunities available. In contrast, when asked how they recruit people for activity, one chair of a low-engagement site in People for the Environment noted that they have a volunteer sign-up sheet on their website. When asked how effective that sign-up sheet is, he said, "Not very, but I think the main problem in the past has been that the person, that is, our membership chair, is the person to whom those filled out forms went. I think that person was not very effective in sending information out to people so they would see the website." This chapter built a website, but found that it was not useful unless people were directed to it. Unfortunately, they did not have the leadership resources needed to develop a plan for directing more traffic to their website.

Without leaders responsible for mobilizing, the low-engagement chapters exacerbated their recruitment problems by relying only on the most passive list-building activities in the first section of table 5-1. It became a vicious cycle, however, because the more passive the recruitment strategies, the more likely the chapter was to struggle with problems of too few activists or leaders. Without building an adequate prospect pool, they did not have the resources to engage in transformational organizing. Without the organizing, they could not build the prospect pool. They became trapped, constantly feeling like they did not have enough volunteers, and unable to get to scale. For example, one leader in People for the Environment describes the situation as follows:

> [T]his year, it's [a major] anniversary of [our local organization] and we are planning to have a big social gathering... [but] we're having trouble finding people to energize over it. I'm ending up organizing this with a fellow who is a chair of the development committee because nobody else seems to want to take charge of it. So this has been kind of a problem that we've had, that a lot of these ideas that we've had have just kind of sat there and languished because we don't have anybody who is willing to take charge.... [We're] just barely making quorum [for our leadership meetings]. That is not exactly what we would like to be able to do. We would like to have 100% participation.

This chapter struggled to find activists who were willing to take responsibility for outcomes. As they moved up the activist ladder, the numbers of people they could find to fill positions dropped precipitously, since they were relying primarily on people who self-selected into those positions. They did not actively cultivate the activist tendencies of those within the chapter. When asked how they tried to recruit activists for different responsibilities, the same leader replied,

> Basically, we try to ask around and ask people who we know if they know of anybody.... I've also started putting a little blurb on our website for volunteer positions. That's kind of new. I just started it recently and I don't know that there's a whole lot there at the moment other than the volunteer treasurer's position, which has been vacant for a while. And then there's a chair of the personnel committee, and that position has been vacant for a while, too. So, it's been very hard to recruit new volunteers.

The strategies for activist recruitment she describes are very passive. Essentially, they post advertisements and hope that the appropriate people will find them. As a result, they often lacked the activist capacity to do the kinds of activities they wanted, and were unable as a chapter to be as active as they desired.

In contrast, the high-engagement chapters approached building a prospect pool as a process of building relationships to maximize the downstream effects of any mobilizing work they did. They put their energies into building relationships with new members and potential activists, instead of focusing energy only on crafting the right message, or designing the right event that would resonate with people's interests. The focus on relationships emerges in a comparison of people who report being recruited for face-to-face action by leaders in People for the Environment. Face-to-face activity has long been recognized as an important source of relationship and community building. Warren discusses this as the hallmark of organizing techniques in the Industrial Areas Foundation, and scholars such as Jim Jasper and Francesca Polletta argue that it is through interpersonal interactions that associations are able to develop the collective identities they need to generate activist commitment.[11] Figure 5-2 shows differences in the percentages of people from high- and low-engagement chapters who were recruited for face-to-face activity

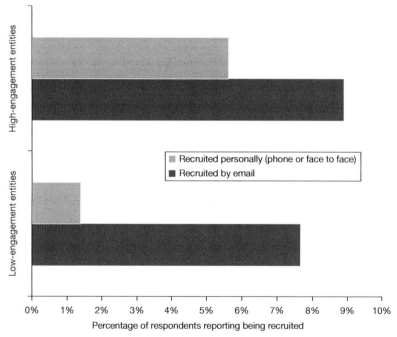

Figure 5-2. Percentage of Respondents Recruited by Email, Phone, or Face-to-Face Activity in High- versus Low-Engagement Chapters in People for the Environment

11. Polletta and Jasper 2001; Warren 2001.

using email, phone, or face-to-face methods. The graph shows that high-engagement chapters did more recruitment for face-to-face activity in general. After being a member for one year, only 9 percent of respondents from low-engagement chapters in People for the Environment reported being recruited for any face-to-face activity, as opposed to 14 percent in high-engagement chapters. Low-engagement chapters were hardly asking their members to participate in any in-person activity. Even when recruiting people for face-to-face activity, leaders in high-engagement chapters were more likely to reach out to people in more personal ways, via phone or in person. In low-engagement chapters, 7.6 percent of people reported being recruited for face-to-face activity via email, none by phone, and only 1 percent in person. In high-engagement chapters, a comparable percentage of respondents reported being recruited by email (9 percent), but far more people reported being recruited by phone (4 percent) and through face-to-face contact (2 percent).

The differences in recruitment are smaller in the National Association of Doctors. While respondents from high-engagement chapters did report being recruited more than respondents from low-engagement chapters, the differences were not statistically significant. Nonetheless, a comparison of practices between high- and low-engagement chapters in the National Association of Doctors reveals telling differences. A leader from one of the low-engagement chapters described his attempts to mobilize people by essentially sending them emails to events he was planning for other purposes.

> [The National Association of Doctors] was providing a nice infrastructure for us [the field leaders] to have the email lists. So when I would have events, say an event was with Move On or with the Democratic Party or whoever we were working with at the time, it was nice to be able to do a blast email and that kind of thing to contact people and let them know what was going on.

Leaders from high-engagement chapters had different strategies. One leader says,

> I find that when I want to mobilize people I may send out a notice that this is going to happen, and I usually find I don't get very much response

when I send it to the whole group. But then I start hitting individuals, getting to know them and asking them personally and then that works much better. It's much more effective to get people. All of sudden they'll do it and they hadn't even looked at the big one.

When the leader from the high-engagement chapter realized that her email notices were not working, she started reaching out to people more personally, trying to build a relationship with them before asking them to take action. The leader from the low-engagement chapter, in contrast, simply relied on email and did not take much notice of how effective or not it was. High-engagement chapters focused more on ongoing learning and innovation to find strategies that worked, and emerged with more relational approaches to mobilization.

Another downstream effect that high-engagement chapters sought to create was a sense of community, or social capital. Leaders of high-engagement chapters worked intentionally to build a sense of community among members and supporters such that even people who were not in relationships with each other felt that they were part of a larger community. Their hope in creating this sense of community was to create a situation in which people's commitment to activism was not borne solely of their commitment to the issue but also their commitment to the people around them. As Debbie, one of the leaders in the National Association of Doctors said,

I think one thing that's felt unique and always sort of raises eyebrows about this organization is that it is basically a volunteer-led and run organization. All of us are here on our free time and a lot of us foot the bill for our own plane tickets to D.C.... Ultimately, at the end of the day, the reason all of these people came together is not just for [health policy]. The reason that I totally believed in the strength and value of our organization is because it's a whole bunch of people who are on conference calls in between taking care of their children and taking care of their patients. So often we're on a conference call and you get a text from someone who says sorry, "I'm with a patient I can't come." I think having that grounding reminds us why we are here. If this other person who is so busy can do it, I can do it too.

As activists' commitment to the voluntary activity inevitably flagged, people in high-engagement chapters reported thinking of their relationships with the people around them, feeling motivated to continue working because they did not want to let their peers down. People in low-engagement chapters tended to react by thinking of their commitment to the issue, trying to push themselves to say that their work on environmental or health issues was absolutely necessary. Given the small difference that any one activist's actions makes, however, these issue commitments were sometimes not enough. A volunteer in a low-engagement entity in People for the Environment says,

> Yeah, they ask me to do stuff all the time. But I always think to myself, "Do they really need me?" It's like, "Will my doing this one little thing really change the environment?" Or sometimes I want to do it, but then I forget or the email gets lost or I can't find the message.

Because this person's activism was not grounded in a set of relationships or a broader community, he often found ways to make excuses for his work. He did not feel that it would matter or make a difference. There was no one counting on him to take this action. Other life commitments took priority and then he lost the information he needed. His reaction contrasts to Debbie's reaction above, who often felt that she could not shirk on her activism because she would let other people down.

To create this sense of community, high-engagement chapters often strategically integrated offline mobilization techniques with online tools that augmented the power of offline efforts. The National Association of Doctors, for instance, frequently invited people to join their online activities through online webcasts or other live streaming media. In doing so, they would create maps showing where in the country people were tuning in, so that an individual doctor watching an event in Washington DC from her office in Kansas could see how many people around her were also watching. At the event itself, they would take comments, questions, and feedback from the online community, such that people who were not able to be in Washington DC nonetheless felt like they were part of something larger. Essentially, high-engagement chapters found ways to simulate through online work the relationships and community they created in offline activity. Pat, a staff member with a high-engagement chapter in People for the Environment, describes their approach with Facebook:

> PAT: Facebook has been pretty helpful [in recruiting people] when Facebook is used well.... [When we first started using it,] we partnered with groups that ha[d] really good Facebook networks set up. That's been really successful.
> INT: So when you say "used well," what do you mean?
> PAT: I think it's when you've built a really vibrant Facebook community where people feel connected to each other or to something. So there's lots and lots of people with lots and lots of friends, and you are regularly posting and sort of creating that online community. Then when you point them in a certain direction to do something, you have lots of people already feeling like they want to do it.... But, it takes a lot of time to do that, and so we have to support it. We have volunteers who were really well trained on it and they can do it, but again, we need that training and support to do that.

Pat was primarily focused on building a community online, recognizing that online tools can have downstream effects supporting the work the association does elsewhere. The online tools gave Pat a broader reach than she might have with only face-to-face outreach, but she used those tools to push people toward offline activity. Doing so helped her continue to build the relationships and community she needed to foster collective identities. Organizers like Pat would treat online conversations as more than just a billboard. They would use them to make people feel connected to something personal.

The high-engagement chapters thus used a broader array of strategies and were more likely to rely on the strategies that had downstream effects for the association as they mobilized. Often, creating these downstream effects depended on building relationships with volunteers because relationships are an important source of motivation and transformation.

HOW EFFECTIVE ARE THE TACTICS ORGANIZERS USE?

Many of the tactics organizers used to mobilize activists are characterized by their attempt to lay a relational basis for future work. The use of relational tactics by organizers is consistent with a large and growing body of evidence about the power of relational recruitment. Previous research indicates that emphasizing social connections should make it more likely that people will get involved.[12] The more personalized the form of outreach, for instance, the more likely people are to be activated for action. Door-to-door canvassing is generally far more effective in getting out the vote than phone calls, and phone calls are more effective than emails.[13] Other social dimensions of campaign and association outreach also matter. Giving people a sense that they will be held accountable among their neighbors for whether or not they take action can boost turnout rates,[14] as can drawing on people's social networks and engaging them in interpersonal conversations. Klein, Becker, and Meyer argue that associations that are able to build relationships with and among members characterized by reciprocity, high levels of support, and frequent opportunities for interpersonal interaction are more likely to generate committed members.[15] Reciprocity, contact, and support are some of the factors Cialdini argues increase the sense of social connectedness, thereby making people more responsive to requests for action.[16] Across a wide range of studies and academic disciplines, research shows that appealing to people's social motivations can make it more likely people will take action.

One relational strategy commonly used by organizers in the study was to reinforce people's social identities. Building people's self-concepts as activists has particular potential to create downstream effects for the

12. Cialdini 2001; Klein, Becker, and Meyer 2009; Musick and Wilson 2008.

13. Green and Gerber 2004, 2008.

14. Gerber, Green, and Larimer 2008.

15. Klein, Becker, and Meyer 2009.

16. Cialdini and Goldstein 2004.

association. Previous research shows that individuals will go to great lengths to act consistently with identities they have established.[17] If the association can mobilize people in ways that built these identities, they would be more likely to be able to draw on them in the future. Many of the high-engagement chapters in the study, thus, used identity reinforcement as a tactic in mobilizing.

Three field experiments I conducted with the National Association of Doctors and People for the Environment demonstrate the ability of these identity-based strategies to help the association reach its transactional goals.[18] These three studies found that efforts to reach out to potential activists that reinforced their identities as activists were more effective in recruiting people to action than other approaches. Previous scholarship has shown that civic and political action can be one way for people to identify and express social identities.[19] One reason why social interactions may be such a powerful influence on participation is that they provide a context within which people can express their social identities. In these studies, the National Association of Doctors reinforced activist identities among people in the treatment groups by sending emails that said things like, "I know you're the kind of person who cares" and referencing their past activity. Then, the National Association of Doctors asked people to sign an online petition, sign up to attend a conference, or reach out to recruit others. In the context of the study, the decision to sign the petition, attend the conference, or reach out to others then became a way for the person to express their social identity or be part of a community of activists. When compared to people receiving standard messages with no reference to particular identities, relationships, or communities, people receiving the social identity messages were at least twice as likely to sign the petition, to click on the links to find out more about the conference, or reach out to recruit others.

17. See Rogers, Fox, and Gerber 2012 for a summary of this research in the context of political participation.

18. The experiments are described in more detail in Han 2014.

19. Rogers, Fox, and Gerber 2013; Garcia-Bedolla and Michelson 2012.

Put together with a long tradition of research on the relational basis of human action, these studies show that online mobilizing tactics can be used to achieve transactional outcomes and create some of the downstream benefits that make transformational organizing more likely. When people received emails referencing particular activist identities, they were more likely to respond. These experimental studies thus reveal a few examples of ways associations can create appeals that simultaneously help an association achieve its transactional goals and lay the foundation for future organizing.

CONCLUSION

Civic associations have to take their work to scale to win the advocacy outcomes they desire. In mobilizing people for civic and political activity, a primary function of civic associations is to differentiate those within the general population who sympathize with their cause from those who do not. In addition, even among those who have demonstrated themselves to be sympathizers by joining, the association must differentiate those who are willing to actually engage in activism from those who are not. This process of identification and differentiation—or "list-building"—helps the association develop the most promising pool of prospective activists and achieve its transactional goals. A number of factors influence whether or not an individual chooses to self-identify as a sympathizer and, further, whether she chooses to take action, so the size and composition of this prospect pool is constantly in flux. Associations like People for the Environment and National Association of Doctors are hence engaged in a constant process of outreach, identification, and list-building as a way of taking their work to scale.

This chapter reviewed the kinds of strategies these two associations used to engage in transactional mobilizing. Remarkably, the strategies used across both associations and across the local chapters were very similar. They ranged from extremely passive forms of marketing that merely hoped users would come to them, to more aggressive forms of outreach designed to identify people who would respond to short, pointed requests. The most passive forms of marketing included setting up websites and Facebook pages, and posting flyers in the hopes that interested people would turn to those sources to seek out information. More aggressive forms of outreach included emails, phone banks, and canvassing designed to identify sympathetic activists. As the lists were generated, the associations then sent a continual stream of emails and other messages to people on the list, in the hopes that some people would take action, identifying themselves as people willing to engage at higher levels of the activist ladder.

Many scholars have studied the strategies associations use to identify and activate prospective activists through transactional mobilizing. Studies of volunteerism examine strategies used to recruit and retain volunteers in a wide range of organizations, including service organizations, recreational groups, neighborhood organizations, and political groups.[20] A growing body of research on get-out-the-vote (GOTV) strategies examines mobilization in political campaigns,[21] while research on social movements and social movement organizations examines mobilization in these contexts.[22]

We have less research on the downstream effects of these mobilization strategies. Yet, thinking about these potential downstream effects is what differentiated the organizers from the mobilizers. Both mobilizers and organizers used these list-building and outreach strategies. Mobilizers differed from organizers in that they often did nothing else. Mobilizers would welcome people who were interested in becoming activists at any level and give them opportunities to get involved—but if someone showed no initial interest in doing so, or was not a self-starter up this ladder, the association itself did not do anything to try to push them to higher levels. They focused only on the transactional outcome, in other words. Organizers, in contrast, anticipated the possibility of transforming people's capacities in the future. They would try to lay the foundation

20. e.g., Musick and Wilson 2008.

21. e.g., Green and Gerber 2004, 2008.

22. Snow and Soule 2010; Snow, Soule, and Kriesi 2007.

for building future relationships with people from the start. These organizers would seek to achieve their transactional goals in ways that laid the foundation for future organizing. Often, they would reach out to people in ways that made salient the social motivations that could later serve as the basis for organizing. By blending mobilizing with organizing, in other words, these high-engagement entities sought to do transformational organizing to build their core of activists and leaders—but to do it at scale.

6

Conclusion

The strength of American democracy has always been premised on the active participation of an engaged citizenry. Democracy works when ordinary people join together to advocate for their interests in the political arena. Yet many people do not participate. Multiple scholars have chronicled the low and unequal rates of participation in American public life.[1] When people lack equal opportunities to exercise voice, or when people disengage from politics, distorted and unequal political outcomes can emerge.[2] Participation is crucial to making democracy function, but generating participation is hard.

Civic associations play a crucial role in making democracy work because they help cultivate people's inclinations for civic and political action. People can learn to be activists through role models, conversations around the dinner table, participation in catalyzing political events, or myriad other avenues.[3] Many of these pathways to action are the result of episodic biographical circumstances. Participation in civic associations, however, is not. Over 60 million American adults a year report participating in civic associations,[4] making them an important lever for

1. Schlozman, Verba, and Brady 2012.

2. See, e.g., Hacker and Pierson 2010.

3. See Teske 1997a, 1997b and Munson 2009 for studies of these pathways.

4. US Department of Commerce 2009.

democratic revitalization. By better understanding the way that civic associations can—and do—foster the participation of ordinary citizens in American political life, we can better understand how to generate more robust participation in public life.

This book has examined the strategies 12 local civic organizations use to engage people in civic and political activism, and to develop democratic leaders. I differentiate between transactional mobilizing, or strategies intended to activate people already motivated for action, and transformational organizing, or strategies intended to cultivate people's motivation, skills, and capacities for further activism and leadership. I show that particular associational practices can influence the extent to which associations are able to get people involved, and keep them involved over time. Activism and democratic leadership are not just functions of people's demographic characteristics, the community in which they grew up, or other biographical factors—the kinds of experiences they have within the associations they join matter as well. Understanding the distinctions between different strategies for engagement is important for associations seeking to make strategic choices in a complex political environment, and scholars seeking to understand how these associations foster activism.

This chapter summarizes the findings from the book with particular attention to the contributions it makes to both scholarship and practice. I also discuss the applicability of the findings from this book to other civic associations, and conclude with thoughts on remaining scholarly and practical challenges. Although important limitations to the present study exist, the findings provide important insights into our understanding of how civic associations influence activism, develop leaders, and thus contribute to democratic life.

CONTRIBUTIONS TO SCHOLARSHIP AND PRACTICE

Political parties, campaigns, and civic associations spend millions of dollars each year to develop innovative strategies to engage more people in political activism. Nowadays, more of these associations are turning to social science to help develop and hone better tactics for engagement. Yet, particularly in thinking about how these tactics cohere into a broader strategy, much of the work these associations do is still based on intuition. This book combines unique data from rigorous fieldwork and from field experiments to uncover some of the broad strategic models contemporary civic associations use to engage their members in action.

Democratic organizations—civic associations, political parties, electoral campaigns, and the like—have two main resources: money and people. There is a plethora of research on the ways in which these associations raise and use their financial resources,[5] but more research is needed on how they develop and deploy their human resources. Most of the research thus far has been about quantity—the numbers of people who get involved and strategies that can be used to increase the quantity of involvement. This book focuses not only on quantity but also on quality. How can democratic associations cultivate engagement that is both broad (quantity) and deep (quality)? I argue that just as certain financial investments can have increasing returns for the association, investing in people can also have increasing returns in terms of an association's ability to increase its breadth and depth of activism. By expanding the scope of study, this book makes several important contributions to scholarship and practice.

First, for practitioners, clarifying the distinction between mobilizing and organizing can hopefully make some strategic choices clearer. As discussed in chapter 3, strategic choices are often the product of the context in which they arise, structures that are already in place, the individuals who are making the decisions and the histories they bring to the table, and association narratives that interpret what the association has done in the past and why it did (or did not) achieve its goals. The associations I observed sometimes fell into a pattern of choosing mobilizing or organizing without having clear theories of change in mind, or clear explanations for why they were adopting particular strategies. Instead, their patterns arose by happenstance, depending on the resources available to them, the narratives they created about what worked, and so on. This

5. e.g., Schlozman and Tierney 1986; Walker 1991; Baumgartner and Leech 1998.

book attempts to clarify mobilizing and organizing in such a way that associations can make clearer, more-conscious choices about when and why they might opt for one strategy over another.

Second, the book highlights the important role that civic associations and other democratic organizations can play in cultivating civic and political action. When Tocqueville observed nineteenth-century American democracy, he observed that civic associations were critical to democracy because they acted as "schools of democracy," equipping people with the capacities they needed to be active citizens. People are not, in other words, born activists. Instead, their potential for activism is cultivated over time, through biographical experiences.[6] Civic associations can play a crucial role in this process. Through associations like the National Association of Doctors and People for the Environment, people can learn skills, acquire relationships and networks, and develop the motivations they need for civic and political action.

Researchers and practitioners alike have often overlooked the potentially transformational role civic associations play in cultivating people's activism. Much of the research on political participation has focused on the idiosyncratic characteristics that make someone more likely to take action. As a result, there is a good sense of the fixed demographic characteristics that make participation more likely, but less is known about the ways that democratic institutions (like civic associations) can cultivate activism.[7] In contemporary practical politics, the piercing focus on micro-targeting[8] or widespread attention to digital tools without thinking about the downstream effects those tools have belies an assumption that democratic organizations should focus on mobilizing people, without organizing them for action.

When people have focused on civic associations, some conventional wisdom has suggested that associations inspire activism through charismatic leadership, better messaging, or simply by operating in politically

6. Teske 1997b; Han 2009.

7. Fiorina 2003; Aldrich 1997; Brady 1999.

8. Issenberg 2012; Hillygus and Shields 2008; Kreiss 2012.

friendly communities. This book turns that conventional wisdom on its head. As shown in chapter 2, the kinds of people joining high-engagement chapters were not that different from those joining low-engagement chapters. Similarly, the kinds of communities in which they worked were not distinct from others. So what was different about the high-engagement chapters? High-engagement chapters differentiated themselves not by luck or charisma, but by a set of practices used to engage people in activism. These practices were designed not only to reach the broadest possible pool of potential activists but also to invest deeply in a subset of those activists and transform them into civic leaders. These organizers actively cultivated their members' motivation to engage in higher levels of activism by building relationships with their members, developing a sense of community, and structuring work in ways that built ongoing commitment.

Third, the book looks at strategies for first getting people involved and also for keeping people involved. In studying associational involvement, more research has examined the question of why people join, or first get involved.[9] There is less work on why people stay involved over time. Although the kinds of things that get people involved are likely to overlap with the kinds of things that keep them involved, we cannot assume they are the same. Some research has shown that many people join associations for episodic, biographical reasons, but deepen their commitment based on experiences had within the association.[10] This book hones in on the question of what kinds of experiences are most likely to keep people engaged over time.

Mobilizers and organizers use different strategies for keeping people involved over time. As discussed in chapters 4 and 5, because mobilizers focus on activating people's latent interests for participation, they are not concerned with pushing them up the activist ladder. Instead, they let people self-select onto different rungs of the ladder. Their strategies for maintaining involvement are largely limited to creating participatory

9. Olson 1965; Walker 1991; Baumgartner and Leech 1998.

10. Munson 2009.

opportunities for members that will appeal to their interests. Organizers, in contrast, are interested in cultivating people's desire and ability to act, and thus use strategies that build relationships, create a sense of community, and otherwise bring people into contact with other volunteers and leaders within the association. The goal is to help people build commitment to other people, not only to the issue at stake, such that people are more likely to stay committed to action.

Fourth, the book makes a distinction between members and leaders, and examines the sources of leadership. Some scholars have called for increased attention to the role that leadership plays in civic associations,[11] but there has been only limited empirical work in this area.[12] Yet leaders are the key decision-makers in what an association does and how it does it. Organization leaders deliberate over and select group structures, strategies, and tactics,[13] shape collective action frames,[14] and identify opportunities and mobilize resources.[15] They do the work required to launch and sustain programs, engage active participants, and expand recognition.[16] Leaders are vital to civic associations, but very little work has examined the sources of leadership in these associations.

Leaders, like activists, are not born but made. As argued throughout the book, a crucial distinction between mobilizing and organizing is the extent to which the association seeks to cultivate the capacities of the people it is trying to engage. Ganz argues that organizers work "by identifying, recruiting, and developing leadership at all levels. This leadership forges [an associational] community and mobilizes its resources, a primary source of [associational] power."[17] Developing leaders, in other

11. Ganz 2009, 2010; Morris and Staggeborg 2007.

12. Dorius and McCarthy 2009; Baggetta, Han, and Andrews 2013.

13. Ganz 2009; Morris 1984; Polletta 2002.

14. See Morris and Staggenborg 2004.

15. Zald and McCarthy 1987.

16. Robnett 1996; Andrews et al. 2010; Rothenberg 1992; Smith, Carson, and Alexander 1984; Skocpol, Ganz, and Munson 2000; Baggetta, Han, and Andrews 2013.

17. Ganz 2009, 510.

words, is the core practice through which organizers work. Chapter 4 describes some of the ways they develop leaders, including training, coaching, and constant reflection. By developing relationships with the activists they are seeking to cultivate, organizers create a "reflective praxis" through which people develop the capacities they need to take on leadership roles.[18]

Finally, through the observational and experimental data presented, the book identifies some concrete strategies and organizing principles that civic associations can use to engage activists and develop leaders. Table 6-1 summarizes those strategies and principles, which are all described in further detail in chapters 4 and 5.

Whether building the prospect pool or developing leaders, high-engagement chapters in the study differentiated themselves through a set of strategies designed to ensure both broad and deep outreach to members. To build their prospect pools, high-engagement chapters had a designated leader who was in charge of recruitment, who could think proactively about ways to reach new people and identify new groups of potential supporters. Instead of waiting for people to come to them, high-engagement chapters actively reached out to people, trying to get them to attend events, sign up, check out the website, or otherwise engage with the chapter. They used a wide range of tools to reach out to people, from more passive tools like websites to more active tools like asking existing members to reach out to their friends.

In addition, throughout the recruitment process, high-engagement chapters sought to engage people in collective, not individual action. They tried to build relationships and create a sense of community with the prospective activists, to create a context within which they could push these people to engage in further activity. Several field experiments verified the efficacy underlying these strategies. Reaching out to people in ways that let them know the chapter is aware of their values and past activities simulates a relationship and makes it more likely that people will get involved. Reaching out to new members to welcome them creates a sense

18. Warren 2001.

Table 6-1. PRACTICES DISTINGUISHING HIGH-ENGAGEMENT ORGANIZATIONS
FROM LOW-ENGAGEMENT ORGANIZATIONS

Function	Strategy	Data Source
Building the prospect pool	Have a leader responsible for recruitment	Comparative Case Studies
	Be proactive about driving people to marketing sites (website, Facebook, etc.)	Comparative Case Studies
	Use individual and functional outreach tools (phone banks, friend to friend outreach, house meetings, etc.)	Comparative Case Studies
	Build relationships with prospective activists	Comparative Case Studies
	Reinforce people's identities as activists	Field Experiments
	Let people know the organization knows what they have done in the past	Field Experiments
Developing leaders	Engage people in interpersonal activities that bring them into contact with others	Comparative Case Studies
	Give volunteers strategic autonomy in their work	Comparative Case Studies
	Create a sense of community among members	Comparative Case Studies
	Reach out to new members	Field Experiments
	Engage people in campaigns/teams	Comparative Case Studies
	Use stories	Comparative Case Studies
	Engage people in reflection about their work	Comparative Case Studies and Field Experiments
	Provide training, coaching	Comparative Case Studies

of community that makes it more likely that the new members will take action.

High-engagement chapters also used a distinct set of strategies when they were developing leaders. They engaged people in interpersonal activities, so that people would begin to develop commitment not only to the chapter but also to the other individuals within it. They gave them strategic autonomy to exercise their own agency. They also involved people in campaigns and teams that had clear goals and pacing that made people feel like their unique contributions were worthwhile. Finally, they led people in constant, ongoing reflection and dialogue about their work, using stories to help them interpret what they were doing and providing training and coaching that helped people develop their skills, contextualize their work, and develop more commitment. Recognizing the differences between high- and low-engagement chapters and the kinds of practices they use can help other associations strategize about ways to get their members involved.

EXTERNAL VALIDITY

Because the data in this book come from research with two major civic associations, a key question that arises is the extent to which these findings are generalizable to different kinds of associations. What about associations working in different issue areas, with different populations, or from different ideological perspectives? How might the findings from this book differ for associations not working on health or environmental issues, who are not organizing doctors or environmental activists, or who work on the opposite side of the political spectrum? Certainly, further research is warranted to examine more closely the ways that associations' effects on activism and organizing and mobilizing strategies might differ across different populations and issue areas. The fact that I found commonalities in the strategies that high-engagement chapters used across two different issue areas and in six different locations around the country—from the deep South to the northeast to the Midwest and the west—provides some preliminary assurance, however, that basic patterns are shared across civic associations working with different populations and on different issues.

One axis of difference that has not been examined at all in this book, however, is the extent to which association strategies on the political right differ from those on the political left. As noted in chapter 2, both of the associations studied in this book work in progressive politics, thus leaving open the question about the extent to which the findings are generalizable to politically conservative associations. Do civic associations on the right similarly cultivate their members for activism and leadership? How are their strategies similar or different?

To shed some light on this question, I examined some publicly available data sources about conservative civic associations to compare them to the associations I studied. In particular, a number of Tea Party associations make their training materials and resources available online. Although the ideologies espoused by the conservative associations were clearly distinct from the ideologies espoused by the associations I studied, the strategies for engagement had common features. For example, the group American Majority, a nonprofit association dedicated to training conservative activists and candidates, puts out a training manual for grassroots activists called "Effectivism: Activism that Works."[19] In this manual, the American Majority lays out core principles for budding activists to use to build power in their communities.

The "Effectivism" training manual for conservative activists espouses the same practices as the high-engagement chapters I studied, in that it teaches activists to blend organizing with mobilizing. Throughout the manual, American Majority makes the point that "effectivists" should do their work in such a way that they build relationships with potential activists to lay the groundwork for cultivating future activism. The "Effectivism" manual encourages organizers to "Build your coalition in a way that will allow it to continually grow. The impact your coalition will have within your community is directly related to its short- and

19. See manual at http://americanmajority.org/wp-content/uploads/2009/11/2013_Effectivism_manual_FINAL.pdf?submissionGuid=fe5bf790-e5c4-456b-9117-01b640376bbf.

long-term strength." Activists should, in other words, do their work as organizers, so that they are always engaging more people. How should they do that? How do they constantly increase the number of activists in their coalition? "Effectivism" suggests trying to build relationships and create a sense of community. "One of the best ways to solicit votes and identify supporters is to knock on doors and talk with people face to face about the candidate." They argue that canvassing—in contrast to other forms of voter contact online or via phone—is more effective because it is "high impact," "leaves greatest and longest lasting impression on voters," and "engages and includes voters." The interpersonal, community aspect of organizing is critical to the "Effectivist" strategy. "When you get a group together," the authors of the manual write, "make time for socializing." Throughout the manual, American Majority encourages activists to engage in the same kind of relational work that organizers in my study did to increase the likelihood that more people will become engaged in the work of the conservative movement.

At the same time, the "Effectivism" manual also encourages people to blend their organizing with mobilizing techniques. "Be visible within your community and be accessible." Part of engaging more people is casting a wide net through mobilizing techniques. The manual trains people to use online and offline techniques to accomplish this. It explains,

> It's the 21st century. Our forms of communication are probably changing more rapidly than since the invention of the printing press. No, that's not a blanket call for all political activity to migrate to the Internet. In fact, many of the most effective ways of disseminating what you want to say are still counter-intuitively personal and old-fashioned. But to ignore the fact that the advent of 24/7 news, on-demand entertainment, and online information and services has changed the way we live is to bury your head in the sand. Activism must change accordingly. There is no excuse to not be as engaged as you want to be. Be that go-to blogger…. You can draw others to your cause, or dominate the public debate on Facebook or Twitter. Or you can rock it old school and simply show up in person at those regularly scheduled monthly meetings and hearings: take a number, wait, and then step up to the microphone, letting all who are listening or watching on cable know exactly what you think of the seated public servants and their latest plans.

Just as the high-engagement chapters in my study did, this manual encourages conservative activists to cast a wide net to capture as many potential activists as possible. By blending mobilizing with organizing, the manual argues that activists can build the conservative base they need.

Other striking similarities exist. For instance, both the National Association of Doctors and People for the Environment built on training materials developed by Marshall Ganz and the New Organizing Institute, a progressive organization dedicated to training organizers on the Left. A widely used training from these sources teaches people to reach out to and engage others through the use of stories, particularly a three-tiered story about yourself, your community or group, and the urgent need for action. They call it a "Story of Self, Us, and Now."[20] American Majority teaches conservative activists to do the same, but they call it a story of "Me, Together, Do."[21] In this framework, activists should tell stories about themselves, about who they are when they work with others, and what they need people to do. The two frameworks are very similar.

The similarities between activism trainings are not limited to the American Majority or Tea Party organizations. Historical accounts of the rise of the Christian Coalition discuss the importance of the grassroots in building the conservative movement.[22] In an analysis of training tapes for grassroots activists, Lesage describes the steps they outline for people to start a local Christian Coalition chapter and to go from "three to eighty committed members."[23] These steps draw on many of the same mobilizing and organizing strategies as are used by the National Association of Doctors and People for the Environment. First, the Christian Coalition advises activists to develop a prospect pool by drawing on "pre-existing anti-pornography lists and church directories" and using "voter surveys" to identify like-minded people. Once they develop this list, a "core group of activists" invites "400–500 people to a county-wide organizing

20. See, e.g., trainings, http://neworganizing.com/toolbox/organizing-and-leadership/.

21. See training, http://www.youtube.com/watch?v=ZVA6xAJ5Isc&noredirect=1.

22. Wilcox 2000; Diamond 1998.

23. Lesage 1998.

meeting," assuming that about 80 people will show up. Once people show some interest by coming to the meeting, the activists immediately infuse them with responsibility. "At the organizing meeting, people sign up for positions such as running a finance committee, acting as public-affairs liaisons to churches who will set up social action 'mission' committees in each parish (for voter registration, for example), or serving as precinct captains who conduct the strategically important voter-identification surveys." Once people are given responsibilities, they then receive training and support to fulfill their roles.

Lesage argues that the goal of this process for starting a local Christian Coalition chapter is to "create a sense of being enveloped in a conservative community," so that "moral convictions now gain the force of a public voice, if not yet public policy." By creating relationships with others, taking on responsibility, and working to spread the message of the Christian Coalition, people begin to see the possibilities of collective action, thus moving up the activist ladder. Lesage writes,

> Motivating someone else to act on moral concerns which have long concerned you both means that as a local political organizer, you have taken a step to awaken in others a collective sense that change is possible and reassures both of you that you are acting effectively as agents of that change…. In this light, Christian Coalition activism can be seen as creating new "conditions of possibility" for its members. That is, it gives people an historical sense that they are participating in a new kind of politically significant, empowering, religious-conservative community.[24]

Organizing within the Christian Coalition is about creating the conditions that make it likely someone will engage in further activism. It draws on people's moral values and calls them to action on behalf of those values. Like the organizers in the National Association of Doctors and People for the Environment, organizers within the Christian Coalition wanted to create a sense of community, build relationships, give people responsibility, and equip people with the skills and motivations they need

24. See http://pages.uoregon.edu/jlesage/Juliafolder/ChristianCoalitionTraining.html.

to become leaders. The strategies they used were very similar to those in the associations I studied.

A full understanding of the ways in which organizing on the Left and the Right are different from and similar to each other is impossible without a parallel study of conservative associations. Nonetheless, this review of publicly available materials about grassroots activism within the conservative movement indicates that there are many parallels between the work of civic associations on the political Left and Right. The kinds of strategies that work to get people involved appear to be consistent across the political spectrum.

ONGOING CHALLENGES FOR SCHOLARSHIP AND PRACTICE

Through its examination of the role that civic associations can play in fostering activism and civic leadership, the book uncovers several ongoing challenges that remain for both scholars and practitioners. These two groups have much to learn from each other. While scholars can provide insight and data to help answer crucial questions about civic associations and democratic engagement, practitioners can provide perspectives on movement building and civic and political activity in the real world. Together, the two can create usable knowledge that helps build democracy.

First, as noted above, important questions remain about the extent to which findings from this book are applicable to other issue areas, other populations, and other segments of the political spectrum. This book looked specifically at associations seeking to engage doctors in activity around health politics, and citizens for activity around environmental issues. As such, both populations examined in this book were relatively privileged populations, since doctors and those in the environmental movement tend to be better educated, of higher socioeconomic status, and, in the case of the environmental movement, white. How, then, might findings differ among lower income populations, minority populations, or other kinds of communities? Some previous research indicates that poorer people tend to have better understandings of power, but fewer skills for civic action.[25] How might mobilizing and organizing in these populations differ as a result? In addition, further examination of civic associations on the political Right is also warranted. Although there is reason to believe that the core findings are robust across different populations, issues, and ideologies, further study of this question is important.

Second, further research into the causal relationships between association actions and collective action is needed. This book sought to address questions of causality through a comparative research design and a set of field experiments designed to test the principles of organizing found in observational data. Nonetheless, much more work is needed. Many of the interventions examined in this study were relatively brief, designed to examine efficacy of the underlying principles that governed the mobilizing and organizing strategies civic associations used. As a result, the studies do not necessarily mimic the intensive interventions that organizers in the high-engagement chapters tended to make. Further studies examining the short- and long-term effects of more intensive interventions would be useful.

Relatedly, research on the conditions under which different kinds of interventions are most likely to be effective would be useful. What are the conditions under which people are most likely to be open to interventions designed to increase their level of engagement? How can civic associations create the conditions that make it likely that people will be open to relationship building, creating communities, and the like? Studies examining the effect of these kinds of interventions on different populations and under different circumstances can help us answer some of these questions.

Finally, important questions remain about how these strategies can be taken to scale. This study examined the mobilizing and organizing strategies used in local chapters and found that high-engagement chapters combined mobilizing with organizing. Doing the work of organizing people and developing leaders can have enormous payoffs for the chapter—as organizers like Phil from chapter 1 found—but also requires

25. Christens, Speer, and Peterson 2011.

a tremendous amount of patience and dedication. In the contemporary political environment, in which civic associations are often held accountable for immediate results by funders, members, and other constituencies, how can civic associations create the space for organizing? How can they generate and devote the resources needed to build their power base through organizing?

More people say they want to participate than actually do. Anyone who has worked in organizing or mobilizing knows that many more people will pledge to vote, attend an event, or otherwise take action than actually do. To close the gap between intention and action, we need more civic associations mobilizing and organizing people for involvement. To make our institutions of democracy as effective as possible in reaching out to engage people, however, we need to develop a better understanding of how to cultivate activism and democratic leaders.

THE TRANSFORMATIVE POWER OF CIVIC ASSOCIATIONS

A volunteer leader with the National Association of Doctors, Darrell works in his local community but also at the national level. When asked to reflect on his experiences, Darrell discusses how associations like the National Association of Doctors can have a transformative impact on people:

> My expectations when I first [became a leader] were lofty, and I should say that they still are, but my hope was that we would be the type of organization that built a community of deeply engaged physicians that gave them a sense of hope and purpose about collective action, and that generated real changes in our health care system that could benefit doctors and patients. That was my real hope. My hope wasn't that this would be yet another organization with a slightly different slant on… health care policy, but that this would be transformative in terms of how physicians engaged with the health care system, and with the public, and with [elected officials and policymakers]… I think that we have succeeded to different degrees. I think that we have engaged certainly a lot of physicians. I think there are a lot more physicians than

I would have hoped that we would have engaged at this point. I think it also bears mentioning what engagement really means, because for some people engagement is being on an e-mail list; for others it's being a state director, or being on the board, and of course there's everything in between, but I guess when I think about engaged, I think about a sense of real ownership. I think about whether you're on an e-mail list, or whether you're a state director, or whatever, the question is do you feel an allegiance to this organization in the sense that do you feel that this organization represents you in a meaningful way? Do you feel like it makes a meaningful contribution to your life, and to the health care system in this country? And that in my mind is the kind of engagement that I want our organization to have.

Darrell became active in the association because he wanted to be part of something transformative. He did not want it to be just another association, but something that really changed the way doctors engaged in health policy, but also changed the doctors themselves. He wanted to be part of an association that made a "meaningful contribution" to the lives of people who were part of it—and, he feels like the association accomplished those goals.

One of the central findings of this book is that when associations manage to create those transformative experiences for their members, the members are more likely to engage in activism. Thus, when Darrell reflects on the strengths of the National Association of Doctors as an association, he discusses the deep commitment of volunteer leaders.

I'll say that there are a number of things that I think makes [our organization] successful. I think the fact that we work incredibly hard, I think, it cannot be underestimated. I think the number of hours that are put in by people throughout this organization... but it's absolutely insane, but it drives so much of our progress, and it enables us to get more done, like in a week than a lot of other groups can do in a month. So, I think the fact that people sacrifice and dedicate so much time, and work so hard is a huge part of what makes us stand out.

Volunteer leaders devote enormous amounts of time and energy to the association, thus enabling the association to accomplish more of its public goals. Darrell cites this energy as a unique strength of the association, but notes that it is not the key feature that makes it unique. The key feature, he argues, is building an association that gives people real ownership over it.

> But I think that the real thing, I think, that makes this different... has to do with the fact that [we are] a people powered movement, and there just aren't a lot of organizations out there that are truly people powered. What I mean by people powered is I mean like a movement which empowers and engages people in a way that they feel they have ownership over part of the process, where they feel like the change that's being generated in part bears their stamp and is effective, and not to use a cliché, but that it really is change that they can believe in, and change that will bring them back to the organization. That kind of engagement from the group up is not something most organizations have.... Now there are consequences to that, and I think there's a reason that that hasn't been done. It's because in part it's really, really hard to build a people powered movement, but their consequences are that you don't really generate buy-in, and engagement, and ownership, and you don't harness the real potential that could like drive the movement forward.... So, if we're going to fill a unique role, a niche in the future.... I think our true, unique value will come in how we're able to really design and actualize a people powered movement. That's where I think we can add something of real value [for doctors]. I should also say I don't see this as issue based. I don't think that we have claim over one particular issue, whether it's like prevention or primary care, or whatever it might be. I think our unique niche is going to have far more to do with our approach, and our philosophy than with the issue that we focus on, or anything else, or the connections we have, or money, or anything.

In thinking about his experiences with the National Association of Doctors, Darrell highlights the important role that associations can play in cultivating people's activism. Darrell wanted to create and be part of an association that was "transformative," that was able to give people a sense of "hope and purpose" by engaging them in "collective action" and making them feel like they were truly part of a change process. He reflected that creating such an association had clear "consequences"— people had more "ownership" and were therefore willing to commit "insane" hours to the work. Whether people get and stay involved depends in part on the kinds of experiences associations create for them.

Darrell recognizes that the National Association of Doctors draws it power from the people it engages. It is not about the issues around which they advocate or the connections they have. Instead, their power comes from their people. He recognizes that it takes hard work to create an association that truly draws its power from its people, but he also recognizes that is what makes his association powerful.

Civic associations have acted as the bedrock of American democracy for hundreds of years. They help citizens advocate for their interests in the public arena but also bring people together for collective action. By bringing people together, civic associations help people discover new interests, new skills, and new resources that enable them to be active democratic citizens. Through working with others, people discover a common set of interests that they did not recognize when they were working alone. It is this transformative power that makes civic associations so crucial to American democracy.

In recent years, the ecology of associations has been changing. There are older associations like the Industrial Areas Foundation, which have achieved important successes by focusing exclusively on organizing without any mobilizing. At the other end of the spectrum, there have been prominent examples of widespread mobilization, such as the mobilization around the Kony case that happened without any real organizing.[26] The crush of media attention to issues like the Kony case has given rise to more organizations focusing on mobilizing in the absence of organizing. In thinking through their strategies, associations look around and say, "Look at what happened with Kony. Maybe we can achieve our goals through a social media campaign too." In addition, changing funding streams have also prompted more associations to look to mobilizing strategies.[27]

One danger in the shift toward mobilizing without organizing is that people become more segmented and isolated in their concerns, and the democratic skills and capacities of citizenship are not cultivated.

26. Warren 2001; Fung and Shkabatur 2012.

27. Karpf 2012.

Mobilizers focus on activating people's latent motivations; they do not seek to transform their interests or capacities. Thus, people's preferences for the common good do not shift. Organizations emerge that do not have leaders. Through organizing, as Darrell describes, people become transformed in a way that they begin to understand the common good differently and develop the capacity to act on it. They begin to develop the skills and capacities necessary for democratic citizenship, enabling them to become citizens who can exercise real agency in the democratic process.

To confront the challenges of a changing world, democracy needs stronger institutions. A central premise of American democracy is that democratic institutions work most effectively when people exercise their right to be heard. To enable people to put their voices to use, democracy needs organizers. These organizers help people develop their skills, capacities, and interests in ways that support democratic society. Organizers help individuals—and hence associations—develop power in the political process. This book studied two associations that act as both mobilizers and organizers, engaging broad groups of people in civic and political action, but also cultivating a subset of those people for further activism and leadership. Understanding how these associations achieve their goals can help develop concrete strategies for building the engaged citizenry needed to make democratic institutions work.

Methods

This appendix describes the research methods used throughout the study in greater detail. The information here complements descriptions of the research design provided throughout the book, particularly those in chapter 2.

IDENTIFYING NATIONAL ASSOCIATIONS FOR STUDY

At the outset of the study, the first challenge was finding civic associations who were willing to give me access to their internal data and allow me to observe their practices. To identify potential associations for study, I talked with a range of different people active in politics to ask them which membership-based associations might be good candidates. I was interested in finding associations that were truly membership-based, that had a federated national structure, and had variation in the levels of engagement at the local level. I also leveraged my personal contacts to identify other candidates for study. Then, drawing on personal networks whenever possible, I contacted these associations to discuss the possibility of engaging in research with them.

I contacted approximately ten different associations. Three of those associations never returned my emails and phone calls. Among those that did return my messages, three were not interested in participating in the study after our initial discussions. Four associations expressed interest in being part of the study, and we maintained an ongoing dialogue for several months. After several months of talking with staff and volunteer leaders from these associations and learning more about the ways they worked, I selected two associations for study. The other two seemed less appropriate for the study because they did not have adequate internal data on participation at the local level, their local leaders seemed less willing to participate in the study, and the local chapters did not have enough strategic independence from the national association. As discussed in chapter 1, the two associations that I chose in the end complemented each other nicely because they worked on two different types of issues (health and environmental issues) and engaged two different constituencies (doctors and citizens).

ESTABLISHING TRUST, ACCESS, AND RULES ABOUT CONFIDENTIALITY

An early challenge in establishing a research relationship with these associations was to gain the trust of staff and leaders. In some cases, using personal networks to make an initial introduction helped. Once I established personal contact, I spent several months getting to know relevant staff and volunteer leaders in all of these associations to learn more about them and also to develop a level of trust. In these early conversations, they were particularly interested in finding out more about how my work might help them and whether I was someone who understood the kinds of challenges they faced. Having a background in practical politics helped, as I was able to draw on some of those experiences to talk to them about their work. In several instances in this early period, the associations asked me for advice and insight on challenges they were facing. When I was able to summarize academic research to provide useful information for them, their willingness to participate in the study deepened.

When it came time to formalize our working relationship, I developed a written contract with each association. This contract specified the kind of data I would have access to, the general terms of the study, and the rules about confidentiality. In both cases, I was given access to internal databases used to track activist participation within the association, and permission to contact staff and volunteer leaders for interviews. In addition, I had to agree to keep the identities of the national associations confidential, so that other people reading results of the study would not be able to identify them.

Leaders of the national association were also concerned that the names and identities of localities identified as "high-engagement" or "low-engagement" be kept confidential from people outside the association, as well as people within the association. In other words, the national associations did not want people from within the association who might read my study to be able to identify precisely who I interviewed or which local chapters I studied. In part, this was because the local chapters selected for study did not know if they were selected as high- or low-engagement chapters. (Although they might have been able to guess which category they were in afterwards, they did not know the precise research design at the outset.)

This stipulation explains particular choices made in the book, such as the decision to present data in table 2-4 as a series of differences between each matched pair. By presenting the data as differences, it is almost impossible for someone to track down precisely which locality is represented as the high- or low-engagement chapter. If I had presented the data in its raw form (i.e., giving the precise population numbers for Greenville and Clinton), then it would have been easier for someone to identify those localities. In addition, in choosing pseudonyms for the interviewees presented throughout the book, I intentionally did not choose ethnically matched names. For instance, if the interviewee had a Latino name, I did not necessarily choose a Latino pseudonym to match (and vice versa: just because I chose a Latino pseudonym does not imply that the interviewee's real name is of the same ethnicity). In two cases, I also changed the gender of the interviewee.

In exchange for access to the data and internal practices, I agreed to provide each association with a report about my findings at the end of the data collection phase. This meant that I provided a written report about the results of each field experiment at the conclusion of the experiment.

For People for the Environment, I also provided a written report about the Phase I data. For the National Association of Doctors, I provided an oral report in meetings with national leaders.

Throughout the study, I maintained contact with national association leaders and continued to talk to them about work going on in the association. When asked, I also provided advice, or my perspective, on particular strategic challenges they were facing. None of this advice or these conversations were relevant to the local chapters in the study, however, and I did not provide any of this kind of advice to local leaders until the data collection was complete (even in that case, I did so only in the context of sharing findings from the study with them).

Nonetheless, it is possible that the collegial relationship I developed with the national and local leaders biased my findings and my interpretation of the data I was observing. To minimize this possibility, I tried to rely on quantitative data to substantiate my observations whenever possible. For example, the differences in participation in high- and low-engagement chapters reported by members in the one-year follow-up survey in chapter 2 substantiate the differences I was observing qualitatively. In addition, where quantitative data was not available, I tried to triangulate data sources, such that I had more confidence in a finding if I heard it from multiple people across different local chapters. Finally, although they do not touch on all of the findings, the results from the field experiments provide some indication that the practices of the high-engagement chapters are, in fact, distinct.

SITUATING THE NATIONAL ASSOCIATIONS

Interpreting the meaning of this book for other civic associations necessitates an understanding of where the National Association of Doctors and People for the Environment fit into the larger constellation of membership-based civic associations in America. Although the two associations have their own histories and unique ways of working, they share important characteristics with other civic associations. I begin here with a brief discussion to help situate them in the broader landscape of interest

groups, social movements, and other public organizations that seek to engage people in public action.

Focusing on Health and Environmental Issues

The first association, the National Association of Doctors, seeks to mobilize doctors and medical students to get involved in health politics in
their communities. Gallup polling data show that citizens trust their
doctors more than anyone else to provide them with accurate information about health policy—more than they trust researchers, the president
other elected officials, or other potential sources of information. When
doctors get involved, their collective voice can be potent. Yet only 26 percent of doctors report taking political action, even as 91 percent say that
political involvement by physicians is important.[1] This association seeks
to close this gap.

The involvement of physicians in health policy is a particularly useful
issue area within which to study the dynamics of mobilization and organizing. First, health is an issue that touches the lives of all individuals
in very personal ways. Good health is a precursor to other positive life
outcomes, and all people must interact with the health system in some
way over the course of their lives. Second, it is a policy area in which
the government plays a large role, thus making public advocacy around
health issues important. Third, it is an issue area in which we have seen
limited mobilization. Compared to civil rights, the environment, wom-
en's rights, consumer protection, and some other issues, health policy has
seen less citizen mobilization despite the ongoing debates in government.
Much of the mobilization that has occurred in health politics has been
counter-mobilization by groups trying to stop health reform initiatives.[2]
Fourth, a focus on health allows us to study the mobilization of a professional group that has a direct self-interest in the issue. Understanding

1. Gruen, Campbell, and Blumenthal 2006.

2. Quadagno 2006.

the dynamics of physician mobilization in health politics has important normative and policy implications.

The second association, People for the Environment, tries to mobilize citizens around environmental issues. Just as doctors who get involved in health policy debates can be a powerful voice, citizen activism on environmental issues can have a major impact. Many scholars and activists in the environmental movement have argued that more citizen activism is necessary to win the major policy victories that have been eluding the movement in recent years.[3] Yet, despite a wide array of environmental associations seeking to get citizens involved, levels of citizen activism around environmental issues have remained relatively stagnant. People for the Environment is a major national association seeking to rectify this situation by mobilizing more individuals for environmental activism. Its success has varied widely across local affiliates.

The environmental association provides a useful contrast to the National Association of Doctors because it is about mobilizing citizens on an issue in which their self-interest is more diffuse. While an argument can be made that everyone has direct self-interest in protecting the environment, the results of that work are much more distant than they are for doctors taking action around health policy. In addition, mobilizing citizens who do not share a common professional identity presents a distinct challenge from mobilizing doctors. The environmental movement is also often cited as a classic example of the post-material movements that arose in the late twentieth century.[4] It is useful to see how those movement organizations have adapted to the new information environment.

The Broader Landscape of Civic Associations in America

The National Association of Doctors and People for the Environment are specific types of the many different kinds of associations seeking

3. Ehrhardt-Martinez and Laitner 2010; Skocpol 2013.

4. e.g., Berry 1999.

to advocate for policy outcomes in Washington, DC. According to the Washington Representatives Study, these Washington associations represent a wide range of interests, ranging from corporations, trade groups, unions, education, identity groups, and the like.[5] The National Association of Doctors represents a specific occupation, while People for the Environment is a public interest group. According to the same study, occupational associations comprise 6.8 percent of the types of interests represented by Washington groups, and public interest groups are 4.6 percent. Among all of the occupational associations, 48.7 percent represent a professional group, as does the National Association of Doctors, and 23.8 percent of all public interest groups work on environmental or wildlife issues.

Both the National Association of Doctors and the People for the Environment are part of a class of associations that are individual membership-based associations. The individual membership-based civic associations are important cases for study because of the role they have played in American democracy. In his review of research on the relationship between associations and democracy, Archon Fung argues that scholars have focused on six different ways that associations contribute to the maintenance of democracy: (1) associations have intrinsic value in a liberal democracy; (2) they can behave as Tocquevillian "schools of democracy," cultivating the motivations and skills that individuals need to be active democratic participants, and socializing them into democratic activity; (3) associations can act as a check on official power; (4) they can act as a mechanism of improving representation by giving voice to individuals who may not have access to other channels of expressing their views; (5) associations provide a structure for individuals to deliberate with each other and formulate opinions about government action; and (6) in some cases, they can provide a way for individuals to participate directly in governance or policymaking.[6] Associations play multiple, overlapping roles in American democracy and are thus vital to building and maintaining

5. Schlozman, Verba, Brady 2012.

6. Fung 2003.

civic infrastructure. Skocpol, Ganz, and Munson argue, for instance, that more than one-third of the civic associations that encompassed at least 1 percent of the American population between 1776 and 1955 incubated social movements.[7]

CHARACTERISTICS OF THE NATIONAL ASSOCIATION OF DOCTORS AND PEOPLE FOR THE ENVIRONMENT

Civic associations fulfill these roles in American democracy because of classic characteristics that differentiate them from other kinds of organizations: they are membership based, led by elected leaders, and engage in advocacy on behalf of those members. The National Association of Doctors and People for the Environment exemplify all of these characteristics. To do this kind of public advocacy, both the National Association of Doctors and the People for the Environment employ a federated structure common to civic associations in America.[8] Importantly, for the purposes of this study, the local chapters have considerable strategic autonomy, independently deciding what kind of agenda to pursue, and how to reach out to and engage their members.

Public Advocacy

Civic associations make claims in the public arena on behalf of their members. The National Association of Doctors tries to give voice to the concerns of progressive doctors in the policymaking process, while People for the Environment represents the environmental and public health interests of the public.

The National Association of Doctors seeks to give voice to doctors. Although doctors are an extremely well-organized political constituency, physician associations often focus on a relatively narrow set of issues. For

7. Skocpol, Ganz, and Munson 2000.

8. Skocpol, Ganz, and Munson 2000.

instance, one study of professional physician associations in the United States estimated that physicians meet with legislators in Congress (or their representatives) 29,000 times per year, and that legislative staff report that 81 percent of these meetings are devoted to discussing Medicare reimbursement.[9] While many of the doctors and students who belong to the National Association of Doctors are also members of other professional associations related to their practice area, many of them do not consider those associations to represent their views on health care. Thus, they have gravitated toward the National Association of Doctors. A core principle of the association, then, is to represent the views of progressive physicians and medical students better than other physician associations. To do so, the leaders frequently and sincerely seek member input into their decision-making to maintain their commitment to being a membership-driven association.

People for the Environment is a large public interest association dedicated to protection of the environment. It has a classic federated structure with federal, state, and local organizations. The national association runs national campaigns, lobbies the federal government, works on federal elections, and sets overall direction and policy for the association. In 2010–2012, at the time of the study, the national association focused on issue areas including climate change, regulating public health pollutants, protecting wildlife, and developing volunteer leadership around these issues. Their efforts included mobilizing attendance for relevant meetings and hearings, lobbying legislators and local decision-makers, mobilizing citizen actions, and generating media attention for their work.

Voluntary Membership

Unlike organizations that depend on paid employees, civic associations depend on the voluntary activity of their members. Civic associations derive their power from their ability to attract voluntary contributions

9. Landers and Sehgal 2000.

of time, effort, and other resources from their members.[10] Both the National Association of Doctors and People for the Environment are individual-membership based associations. By the time the study was conducted in 2010–2012, both associations had relatively loose definitions of membership. Unlike older civic associations that had strict definitions of membership and clear rituals that demarcated those who were members from those who were not, many modern civic associations loosened their membership rules to allow anyone who had affiliated with them in any way to be a "member." This loosening of membership rules was one way for associations to adapt to the modern technological environment, in which people could click a button to take action with an association like the National Association of Doctors or People for the Environment even if they were not official members.[11] Instead of disregarding these action-takers because they had not formally joined the association, both the National Association of Doctors and People for the Environment embrace them.

Both associations reach out to their members in a variety of ways. The way individual membership-based civic associations in America engage people in civic and political action has been changing as the information environment in which they operate has shifted. Some argue there has been a shift toward more episodic events and activities, as opposed to long-standing rituals and routines.[12] Instead of asking people to come to monthly meetings or annual dinners, associations are more likely to engage people in events and activities targeted toward specific campaigns, issues, or problems. The National Association of Doctors and the People for the Environment both modeled this kind of activity.

During the time of the study, the National Association of Doctors recruited members primarily through online technology. Once people are on the National Association of Doctors's "list," they are counted as members. People can join the list by taking an action (such as signing a petition

10. Knoke and Prensky 1984; Smith 2000.

11. Karpf 2012.

12. Bimber 2003; Karpf 2012.

or responding to another action alert from the National Association of Doctors), signing up on the website, attending an event, contacting one of the leaders, or joining the group through Facebook and other social networking tools. Much of the association's list is built by recruitment through existing social networks among physicians. Once a person becomes a "member," they begin to receive the National Association of Doctors's emails, which generally amount to approximately two emails per week. These emails asked people to take actions such as signing letters and petitions, donating money, hosting or attending house meetings, organizing and attending town hall meetings to give doctors the opportunity to talk about health reform with audience members, contacting their legislator to express support or opposition to legislation, or speaking with local media about health issues. If people do not wish to remain on the list, they can ask to unsubscribe. In the two years preceding the beginning of the study, the unsubscribe rate was 12 percent. Field organizers on the ground supplemented this work with their own outreach in their local communities. Some 61 percent of members had taken just one action, which is the action they had to take to "join" the association, while 17 percent had taken two actions, and 19 percent had taken three or more actions.

People for the Environment offers multiple pathways to membership that include building a list online, direct mail, telemarketing, paid canvassers, and activities organized by its local chapters. Members can join in multiple ways, including taking an action online or attending an event sponsored by the People for the Environment. An internal report in 2010 suggested thinking about activism within People for the Environment as falling into one of six buckets. The first bucket involves activity that takes only one to two minutes to complete and is primarily about self-affiliating with the association through a social network site (i.e., "Liking" the association on Facebook). Activities in the second bucket also take only one to two minutes to complete but involve signing up as an activist onto an email list or an online community. The third bucket involves online actions that took about three to five minutes to complete and include signing online petitions, contacting elected officials through the association's web interface, or interacting with the association's internal community website, by logging into the site, adding friends, or joining groups. The fourth bucket includes activity that takes 5 to 30 minutes and involves interaction with the offline world, including making phone calls to decision-makers, writing letters to the editor, or other actions that people could take from their home. The fifth bucket includes actions that force users to leave their home, such as attending a canvas, attending a rally or house party, or participating in a phone bank or other event. The final bucket includes actions that take more than five hours like leading an advocacy or social activity. Beyond these buckets, people can also participate in other forms through offline activity within People for the Environment. This activity ranges widely and includes everything from attending a local meeting to hear a speaker, to attending a film festival sponsored by the association, to talking to others about the association's work, to running for elected office within the association.

Governance through Voluntary Leadership

A third distinguishing feature of civic associations is their reliance on voluntary, elected leaders. By electing leaders, civic associations make the leaders directly accountable to the membership. In addition, the voluntary nature of leadership and membership forces leaders to generate commitment and willingness among their members to take action.[13] The need to generate commitment forces volunteer leaders to develop a different set of practices from leaders in associations that have paid staff.

Like many other civic associations, both the National Association of Doctors and People for the Environment are governed by a nationally elected board. They also have volunteer leadership at the regional, state, and local levels. These regional, state, and local leaders are responsible for generating activity in their state or region, and supporting other leaders in the area. In both associations, these volunteer leaders devote enormous amounts of time to the associations and are instrumental in keeping them in operation. They do everything from organizing complicated legal suits,

13. Walton 1985; Kanter 1972.

to organizing citizens to lobby local elected officials and bureaucrats, to fundraising, to organizing events and social outings for members of the local community, to presenting at schools and community fairs on environmental issues, to working with other local civic associations to promote environmental activity in their communities, to reaching out to members to activate their participation, to cultivating others to become civic leaders in their communities, and the list goes on.

Although both associations rely primarily on volunteer leadership, they also have some paid staff. In 2010–2012, the National Association of Doctors had approximately one staff person for every 20,000 members. Given this stark ratio, the association relies almost entirely on volunteer leadership. People for the Environment has approximately one staff person for every 3,000 members. Organizing all of these members, thus, also relies substantially on volunteer leadership. In both associations, all of the staff, including those that work at the national level, report to the elected volunteer leaders.

National, State, Local Structure

Like many classic civic associations, both the National Association of Doctors and People for the Environment organize themselves through a federated structure with national, state, and local affiliates. Multiple scholars have studied civic associations with this multi-tiered structure because it represents an important way for associations to integrate localized action with a broader national framework, and advocate at the local, state, and federal levels of government.[14]

Within the federated structure, the national association shares resources with its state and local affiliates. Members of each association have affiliations with both the national associations and local and state chapters. Both the National Association of Doctors and People for the Environment assign members to local and state chapters depending on their geographic area of residence. In both associations, much fundraising

14. Skocpol, Ganz, and Munson 2000.

occurs at the national level, but state and local affiliates can fundraise independently if they want.

From a strategic standpoint, local affiliates in both associations have considerable autonomy. In the National Association of Doctors, the national association sets national priorities and allows state and local affiliates to develop their own plans for carrying them out. For high-priority campaigns, the national associations sometimes develop a set of metrics for each local affiliate to meet, such as the number of signatures they should generate on a petition or the number of house parties to hold. In these instances, the local affiliates have less autonomy in shaping their own strategies. In other cases, however, the national association would not create any common metrics, allowing each local affiliate to choose what issues areas to work on and how to do it. Much of what they sought to do in weekly conference calls with their field organizers was collect information about what kind of activity was going on at the local level.

In People for the Environment, state and local chapters have considerable autonomy from the national association, with the freedom to set their own advocacy agendas, and raise and allocate their resources independently. Unlike the national association, they often focus on state and local issues and elections in their advocacy and electoral work. They decide what goals they want to focus on, how to pursue them, and whether they want to integrate their work with campaigns run by the national association. The national association often develops national campaigns that operate alongside the work of local affiliates. These campaigns may hire full-time field organizers in localities around the country to organize the local community around environmental issues. Local areas range in terms of how closely these national organizers work with the local volunteer leaders. In some places, the work is very synergistic, such that the work of the national organizers is incorporated into and embraced by the local affiliates. In other situations, the work runs on relatively distinct tracks, such that members who get involved with the national campaign do not necessarily have any interaction with the local affiliate.

This examination of key features of the National Association of Doctors and People for the Environment reveals that they share many of the key features of modern civic associations. They engage in public advocacy, depend on voluntary activity from their members, govern themselves through voluntary leadership, organize their work through a federated structure, and engage their members in a wide range of online and off-line activities. Although both associations have their own idiosyncrasies, they also share features with many other civic associations in American politics.

SELECTING CASES (MATCHED PAIRS OF LOCAL CHAPTERS) FOR STUDY

The process that I used to select matched pairs of local chapters for the comparative case studies in Phase I is described here and in chapter 2.

National Association of Doctors

In selecting areas for study within the National Association of Doctors, I examined internal data on rates of participation within the chapter and consulted with association leaders. We decided to use metropolitan areas as the unit of analysis, despite the fact that the association nominally organizes itself by state. Because much of the association's recruitment is done through word-of-mouth, it relies on pre-existing networks of doctors and physicians. As a result, more members join from urban areas, particularly where there are large hospitals or academic medical centers that have concentrations of physicians and medical students. In addition, most of the offline, face-to-face activities that they sponsor are in urban areas, since that is where they have a sufficient concentration of members. Activism within the less populated regions tends to focus solely on online activities generated by the national association. As a result, there is very little local variation in those areas. Examining differences between metropolitan areas seemed more likely to provide insights into the association's impact on increasing rates of activism.

To demarcate urban areas from each other, I chose hospital referral regions as the unit of analysis. A hospital referral region (HRR) is a geographic area originally defined by the *Dartmouth Atlas of Health Care*. Dedicated to examining geographic variation in health care costs and spending, the *Atlas* divided the country into 306 HRRs. To create the HRRs, they began with the Hospital Service Area (HSA), which defines local health care markets for community-based inpatient care. The country has 3,436 HSAs, which show the geographic area for which each hospital is responsible. Much hospital care, however, is provided by referrals to other hospitals in the area. Thus, the *Atlas* examined where patients were referred for major cardiovascular surgical procedures and neurosurgery to determine the larger HRR. As a result, the HRR shows the "regional market areas for tertiary medical care."[15] The unit of analysis has been used for over 20 years by the *Dartmouth Atlas* and has gained widespread acceptance as a way of geographically defining usage patterns in health care. The advantage of using HRRs in this study over other geographic markers (such as city or county boundaries) is that they are defined based on health care usage patterns, which are more likely to have overlap with physician networks. Thus, even though a hospital may be outside city limits, if its doctors and health care delivery options are closely tied to hospitals and providers within the city, the HRR will capture it. In the main text of the book, I use the term "metropolitan area" to refer to an HRR to minimize the technical jargon.

To select particular areas for study, I began by identifying areas that were particularly strong or weak in terms of historical rates of activism. The best indicator for this was internal association data on the numbers of people who engaged in multiple activities. Because of the way membership is defined within the association, anyone who is a member has engaged in at least one activity. Many people (61 percent, as indicated above) engage in only that activity. Slightly less than half of the members, however, go on to engage in two or more activities. In consultation with association leaders, we decided to examine the rates of people who engaged in more than two activities, since those were the people that the

15. See online Glossary at http://www.dartmouthatlas.org/tools/glossary.aspx.

association considered to be its true activists. These people seemed to consistently read and respond to the messages and calls for action that the association sent. Using this metric, we found that throughout the association, 19 percent of people had engaged in three or more activities, but this activism was not evenly dispersed across the country.

Using this metric, we identified a set of metropolitan areas that were above and below the mean in their ability to engage members in activism. To further narrow the list, I worked with association leaders to identify metropolitan areas in which they had an active field director. We removed areas that did not have active field leadership because variation in activism in those areas was likely due to idiosyncratic factors related to the people who had joined and not anything that the association was trying to do. Finally, we identified pairs of high-engagement and low-engagement metropolitan areas that were geographically matched in terms of demographic characteristics. In other words, we did not want to be comparing activism in San Francisco, California, to activism in Houston, Texas, since the cities were so different in their character. Instead, we wanted to find areas that were similar in their community characteristics, but different in their patterns of engagement. To finalize the list, I conducted interviews with multiple association leaders to get a range of perspectives on the sites on our list and verify that the patterns we were seeing in the data were indeed meaningful.

People for the Environment

Importantly, for the purposes of this study, there is considerable variation across local chapters within the People for the Environment in the extent to which they engage members in both online and offline activism. The national association maintains a database of activists that codes individuals who have participated in some form of activism. In 2010, the state-level chapters ranged from having 0.61 percent to 19.7 percent of their members coded as activists, with one outlier state that had 48.9 percent of their members coded as activists.

To select areas for study within the association, I examined internal association data on rates of participation and interviewed staff and volunteer leaders across the association. We decided to use states as the unit of analysis, so that our analysis could encompass the work of volunteer leaders as well as national campaigns (because the work of the national campaigns tends to focus on the states). Because people can get involved with the People for the Environment through the local affiliates or the national campaigns, we decided to include all of this work in the study.

We then used association data on the percent of activists in each state to narrow the list of states down to 22 potential areas of study. I conducted phone interviews with volunteer leaders, state staff, and national staff organizers in each of these 22 states to verify the numbers reported in the national database, get a sense of the kinds of activities they were undertaking to engage members in activity, and to assess their willingness to participate in the study. All of the states that we interviewed indicated their willingness to participate in the study, so in further narrowing the list of potential study sites, we balanced a range of different criteria, including regional variation across the United States, the size of the membership base in different states, the political climate of the different states, the degree to which leaders within the state could verify the activist numbers in their databases, and the extent to which we could find pairs of high- and low-engagement states that were matched in terms of demographics, geography, and political climate.

ALTERNATIVE HYPOTHESES TO EXPLAIN DIFFERENCES BETWEEN HIGH- AND LOW-ENGAGEMENT SITES

Drawing on previous research, I can provide more detail on the reasons I chose to focus on particular individual and community characteristics in selecting cases for the study. Two prevalent explanations in previous research for why some civic associations are better at engaging people in activism than others have to do with individual and community differences. Perhaps one site simply attracts more people who are ready to become activists than another site—in other words, it attracts a better prospect pool. An individual's choice to participate can be a function of individual characteristics, such as the amount of free time the person has or the extent to which the person grew up in a family that discussed politics at home. If this was the only explanation, the differences in activism may have nothing to do with what the association does and instead be all about who joins. The choice to participate can also be affected by the broader context or society within which the individual is operating. I should not compare levels of participation in Mobile, Alabama, to San Francisco, California, for example, because the two communities are geographically, politically, civically, and demographically so different from each other. Perhaps one site is operating in a more progressive community with more people who are likely sympathizers. Indeed, community differences can be an important explanation for why some sites are better at engaging activists than others.

Researchers have examined the individual traits and characteristics that make it more likely that a person will want to participate. Scholarship has often focused on the importance of individual resources.[16] Education is often associated with higher levels of political knowledge, thus giving people more information about how the political system works and making it easier for them to know how to participate. Money can facilitate certain forms of participation (like donating to campaigns), and it can also afford a person more free time, thus making it easier for them to fit public activity into their life. Possessing civic skills—knowing how to write a letter to a public official, feeling confident about speaking in public meetings and discussing political issues with others—can make public activity more comfortable. People with these resources—education, money, free time, and civic skills—are better able to participate. Participation in public life competes with myriad other activities that could occupy a person's time, including activities that are often thought to be more central to people's lives, such as taking care of children, maintaining relationships with family and friends, and meeting professional obligations. People who have the resources that make participation easier

16. Verba, Schlozman, and Brady 1995; Verba and Nie 1972; Wolfinger and Rosenstone 1980; Rosenstone and Hansen 1993.

are more likely to want to prioritize it over these competing claims on their time.

People must also want to participate. Although motivation has been studied widely by scholars, researchers still lack consensus about how best to conceptualize it in the context of political participation and activism. Within the study of participation, some scholars conceptualize motivation as a composite of the psychological predispositions that make participation more likely. The argument is that people who are more politically interested and feel more politically efficacious are more likely to participate.[17] Others focus less on psychological orientations and more on the kinds of goals and commitments that drive people's participation in public activity. These scholars have created typologies of the instrumental, ideological, and relational motivations that drive political action, and debated the importance of political versus personal goals in generating commitment.[18] Others have focused on the episodic, biographical factors that socialize people to political action, examining the lifelong orientations toward public action that can result from early socializing experiences in the family or school.[19] Still others assert that understanding motivation requires identifying the psychological and neurological processes that move people to take action. This literature tends to focus on the role of emotions in motivating behavior.[20] Motivation is obviously central to political activity—people must want to participate for participation to occur.

Participation is not only a function of individual motivations and characteristics but also of the contextual supply of information about participatory opportunities and access to that information. Research about contextual effects on participation includes the study of how the media, political polarization, political climate, and images of political institutions can affect participation. Much research has examined the effect of

17. Schlozman 2003; Verba, Schlozman, and Brady 1995; Rosenstone and Hansen 1993.

18. Wilson 1973; Han 2009; Miller 2005; Teske 1997b.

19. e.g., Stoker and Jennings 1995; Plutzer 2002; Jennings 1987.

20. Brader 2006; Marcus 2002.

negative advertising on participation, focusing on the relationship between exposure to negative campaign ads and the subsequent choice to
participate.[21] Other research has examined the political climate to see
how it affects participation, finding that factors such as high levels of political polarization or public mood can increase participation.[22] Scholars
have also found that trust in public institutions can mediate people's willingness to get involved[23] and have shown how distal events or images of
political institutions affect more proximal choices to participate.

Some scholars argue that the link between individual and contextual
factors is often through political associations (such as campaigns, civic
associations, etc.). The choice to participate is an interaction between
individual characteristics that influence a person's willingness to get
involved and contextual information about the participatory opportunities that exist. Associations help individuals access the contextual information they need to make their decision. Some scholars argue that one
way to think about it is to imagine a supply-demand framework for understanding political activity. "Demand refers to the potential in a society for
[political activity]; supply refers, on the other hand, to the opportunities
staged by [organizers]. Mobilization brings a demand for a political [ac-
tivity] that exists in society together with a supply of opportunities to take
part in such [activity]."[24] For participation to occur, people have to want
to participate, an opportunity for them to channel those motivations has
to exist, and there has to be a search process that matches those motivations to the opportunities.

To account for these potentially confounding individual and community factors, I selected sites that were relatively matched in terms of things
like region, median socioeconomic status, civic culture, etc. Doing so
allows this study to focus on association factors that differentiate high-
and low-engagement sites from each other. This design allows me to

21. e.g., Ansolabehere and Iyengar 1995; Geer 2006.

22. Mutz 2006; Erikson, MacKuen, and Stimson 2002.

23. Hibbing and Theiss-Morse 2001; Hetherington 2005.

24. Klandermans 2007, 360.

compare the difference between sites that effectively mobilize their members and sites that are less effective in doing so. In addition, it allows me to identify common patterns across two different civic associations.

Contextual and Community Characteristics

Chapter 2 discusses much of the data showing how the matched pairs compared to each other in terms of individual characteristics. Table 2-4 also introduces the data on the community characteristics. I discuss that data further here.

For the National Association of Doctors comparisons, I selected three pairs of cities (six sites total) to be part of the study. Table 2-4 compares these cities to each other, examining a range of civic, political, demographic, and medical indicators (to maintain anonymity, the place names are all aliases). The first thing to note is that the high-engagement chapters—Fairview, Milton, and Oxford—have consistently higher historical rates of activism than their low-engagement counterparts—Madison, Marion, and Jackson, respectively. Fairview and Milton both display historical rates of activism that are slightly more than 4 percentage points higher than Madison and Marion. Oxford's rates of activism far exceed Jackson's, with a 14-percentage-point difference between the two chapters. The high-engagement chapters are all able to engage more of their members in activism than the low-engagement chapters.

In terms of other community characteristics, the cities are not perfect matches of each other, in that no two cities are exactly alike. Yet, on a number of key community characteristics thought to affect political activism within a geographic area, the cities are relatively well-matched. For example, data from the National Center for Charitable Statistics show that the pairs of cities are relatively comparable to each other in terms of the number of civic associations registered. This measure is an indicator of the density of civic culture. Previous research indicates that areas with a denser civic culture are more likely to have higher rates of activism.[25]

25. Putnam 2000; Wandersman et al. 1987; Zeldin and Topitzes 2002.

Yet, the city with lower rates of engagement may actually have a denser civic culture, by this measure, than the city with higher rates of civic engagement. For example, in one pair, the low-engagement city Madison has 580 more civic associations than the high-engagement city Fairview. In another pair, the difference between Milton and Marion is 231, but the high-engagement city has more civic associations. Oxford and Jackson are more like Fairview and Madison, with a difference of 363 associations.

The pairs of cities are also well-matched in terms of political characteristics. A commonly used measure of a geographic area's political liberalism or conservatism is a moving average of presidential vote in the area.[26] I calculated the average of the 2000, 2004, and 2008 presidential votes in these cities and found that cities in each pair showed similar voting trends. The low-engagement city Marion was 4 percentage points less Democratic than Milton, its high-engagement counterpart. Oxford and Jackson differed by less than 1 percentage point, with Oxford (the high-engagement city) being more Democratic. Fairview, the high-engagement city, was 3 percentage points less Democratic than Madison, its low-engagement match. Even though one of the low-engagement cities exhibited a slightly more liberal trend than its counterpart, and another low-engagement city was as about as liberal as its counterpart, neither of these cities were able to engage as many members in activism for this progressive association as their high-engagement counterparts.

Using data from the *Dartmouth Atlas*, I also examined four indicators about the medical community in the area: the number of physicians in the area per 100,000 residents, the number of primary care physicians per 100,000 residents, the number of acute care hospital beds per 1,000 residents, and the percent of patients giving the hospitals high ratings in a 2007 patient satisfaction survey. Here, a few more differences among the cities became apparent. In all three pairs, the high-engagement city had slightly more physicians and more primary care physicians. It is possible that the higher density of physicians makes it easier for the National Association of Doctors chapters to identify and organize activists. Further,

26. e.g., Canes-Wrone, Brady, and Cogan 2002; Han and Brady 2007.

among doctors, previous research has found that primary care physicians are most likely to be active in their communities.[27] Yet, these differences between the cities are not large, and they are not likely to translate into significant differences in hospital capacity or patient satisfaction with hospitals in the metropolitan area.

Some differences do emerge in an examination of the demographic characteristics of these cities. Madison and Marion, the low-engagement cities, are both larger than Fairview and Milton. In the Oxford-Jackson pairing, Oxford, the high-engagement city, is more populous. Fairview is wealthier, better-educated, whiter, and has more foreign-born residents than its low-engagement counterpart Madison. Milton and Oxford are both slightly poorer, on average, than their low-engagement counterparts, but slightly better educated and whiter. It is important to note, however, that the demographic data are taken from the Census, which uses city boundaries to demarcate these areas. The city boundaries do not match the metropolitan area boundaries (HRR's) used to select these sites, and it is possible that the differences between these areas would diminish if we were able to look at the entire metro area. For instance, if we included more of the wealthy suburbs of the low-engagement city in Madison, then it is quite possible that the demographic characteristics would begin to look more similar to those in the high-engagement city.

I also selected three pairs of regions (six states) for study within People for the Environment. Table 2-4 compares the states to each other in terms of levels of engagement and a range of civic, political, and demographic factors. Greenville leads the pack with 19.6 percent of members in the state included in the activist database. Springfield is a close second with 17.5 percent of members in the activist database, and Franklin has 9.23 percent of members in the database (still well above the national mean of 6 percent of members in the activist database). The other states have lower levels of activist engagement. Clinton claims 3.3 percent of members as activists, Salem claims 2.4 percent, and Bristol has only 0.7 percent of members listed as activists in the database.

---

27. Gruen, Campbell, and Blumenthal 2006.

Despite differences in the levels of activism reported in the states, the states are similar to each other on a number of civic, political, and demographic indicators. From a political standpoint, the null expectation might be that the high-engagement areas tend to be more progressive, and therefore more likely to support Democratic candidates. Yet, the data show that is not necessarily the case. A three-election moving average of presidential vote in the states (encompassing the 2000, 2004, and 2008 presidential elections) shows that Greenville, the high-engagement state, is more Democratic than Clinton, but Bristol and Salem, the low-engagement states, are more Democratic than their paired counterparts. In addition, the differences between all of these pairs are small. In other words, patterns of partisanship or political liberalism do not seem to be enough to explain the differences in levels of engagement in these states.

Similarly, the number of civic groups per capita does not show any clear patterns relative to the levels of activism in the state. Clinton, the low-engagement state, slightly surpasses Greenville in the number of civic groups per capita, as does Bristol relative to Springfield. Yet, Franklin, the high-engagement state, surpasses Salem in the number of civic groups per capita. As discussed in the previous section, areas with a denser civic culture are thought to be more civically active and therefore should demonstrate higher levels of activism—yet, that pattern is not consistently borne out by the data here.

Examining the states from a demographic standpoint similarly shows that there is no clear pattern. While the two high-engagement states, Greenville and Franklin, are both more populous than Clinton and Salem, Springfield, the high-engagement state, is much smaller in terms of population than Bristol. The states in each pair are relatively similar to each other in terms of median household income, and it is not clear that higher levels of education necessarily correlate with higher rates of engagement. Greenville is just slightly wealthier and better educated than Clinton, but the differences are relatively small. Franklin and Springfield are slightly wealthier but less well-educated than their low-engagement partners (Salem and Bristol, respectively), on average. Racial diversity within the states and percentage of residents who are foreign-born also does not follow a clear pattern in terms of predicting high- and low-engagement levels. The high-engagement state Greenville has more minorities and more foreign-born residents than Clinton, while the high-engagement state Franklin has a slightly larger white population and a much larger foreign-born population than its counterpart. The high-engagement state Bristol, on the other hand, is much whiter than its low-engagement counterpart, both in terms of the percent of the population that is white and the percent of the population that is foreign-born. The demographic differences between the states, in other words, are very small in many cases. Even when they do diverge, they do not follow a clear pattern.

Because People for the Environment focuses on environmental issues in its work, I also examined some measures of environmental conditions in the state. It is plausible that states that have more acute environmental hazards, for instance, will have more activism around environmental issues because of the localized nature of the problem. Finding precise measures of the environmental condition of a particular state is very hard. Thus, I looked at a variety of different measures. The American Council for an Energy-Efficient Economy (ACEEE) creates a state scorecard rating states in terms of the work they have done on energy efficiency issues. Higher numbers indicate more work on energy efficiency. On this index in 2009, one of the high-engagement states had a higher rating than its low-engagement counterpart, while another high-engagement state had a lower rating, and the third one had a rating that was about equal to its low-engagement counterpart. Another index using historical information considers a broader array of factors. The Green Index is a composite of 256 indicators to profile different dimensions of environmental quality, including "green conditions" and "green policies."[28] All of the states are ranked between 1 and 50 on the Green Index, with lower numbers indicating a "greener" state. The high-engagement states Greenville and Springfield both slightly out-rank their lower-engagement counterparts, but the low-engagement state Salem far outranks its partner on the Green Index. Though not shown in the table, I also examined the Environmental Protection Agency's Toxics Release Inventory data, and

28. Hall and Kerr 1991.

the Energy Information Administration's data. On all of these indicators, the data showed no clear patterns regarding whether high-engagement or low-engagement states have higher reported levels of environmental degradation, energy use, or environmental action. The last environmental indicator examined was the number of environmental groups per capita. This number is slightly trickier to examine because it could be interpreted in several ways. States with more environmental groups may be "greener" and have higher levels of environmental activism overall. Alternately, the density of environmental groups in such states may increase competition for local People for the Environment entities and make it harder for them to engage members. I find that the high-engagement states Greenville and Franklin have more environmental groups per capita than their low-engagement counterparts, but that the low-engagement state Bristol has more environmental groups per capita than its partner. Again, while differences between the states do exist, the patterns are not entirely clear.

This comparison of the cases included in the study on civic, political, demographic, and environmental dimensions shows that although the states are not perfect matches with each other, there is not enough evidence to attribute the differences in engagement between these states to the community characteristics examined here. In other words, it would be of greater concern if all the high-engagement states were more politically liberal, more civically active, wealthier, and "greener"—or if they followed some other consistent pattern across all the states. Instead, I find that across all of these dimensions, there is no clear pattern between high- and low-engagement states, raising the question of what other factors are at play.

STRUCTURAL CHARACTERISTICS OF THE LOCAL CHAPTERS IN THE STUDY

The National Association of Doctors

Structurally speaking, the six sites included in the study were very similar to each other. At the center of each local chapter was a chapter leader, who usually acted as the state director for that area. This person interfaced closely with the national association, working with national leaders to identify opportunities for engaging members and ensuring that the work of the local chapter dovetailed with the campaigns and initiatives spurred by the national association. Surrounding this central leader was an informal group of active participants who worked with the leader to plan, execute, and mobilize activity in the local area. Beyond that, there was little formal structure to the local chapters. They acted largely as loose networks for interested members.

Both Fairview and Madison have very similar structure and leadership. Both cities are led by physicians who were active in civic life and health politics in their cities before getting involved with the National Association of Doctors. Both leaders report getting involved because they felt that having the title of "State Director" would help them "have more influence" and "get others involved." Once they became leaders, both individuals leveraged their existing contacts and the membership list from the National Association of Doctors to develop an informal team of approximately five to six people who constitute an informal group of advisors. This group helps the leaders organize events, interface with the media, and engage others in activity. In both cases, the group is an informal one, however, in which the State Director is at the hub of all the relationships, and there are not consistent relationships that exist between group members.

Milton and Marion are slightly more distinct from each other in terms of their structure. In Milton, a more established leadership team exists that leads the National Association of Doctors's activities in the city. Marion has a less formal leadership structure. There is a central leader who relies primarily on an informal personal network to support his leadership activity. He has a group of about eight doctors in his local city on whom he relies for informal leadership and activism.

Oxford and Jackson are the least structured of the six sites included in the study. Both cities have struggled with leadership turnover for the past several years, including during the study. The national association has tended to recruit leaders to plan particular events or activities in both cities, but has not been able to find someone who can commit to being a long-term leader and build the local chapter. Nonetheless, membership in both cities remains relatively robust. Several volunteers who have been active at the national level have lived in Oxford, and they have been able to leverage their personal networks to maintain a base of relatively active members in the area—despite the fact that none of these members want to commit to a long-term leadership role. Similarly, both cities have strong physician networks from which the National Association of Doctors can generate members. The local chapters in both areas, thus, are run in relatively ad hoc fashion, becoming more active when a willing activist takes the reins, and laying fallow when no one is available. Whenever the national association launches campaigns, however, they do recruit activists from each city to take the helm of particular events and activities. Otherwise, the chapter depends on its informal networks to operate.

People for the Environment

Although the basic structure of the People for the Environment in each state is similar, each state affiliate has considerable autonomy in how it deploys its resources. In addition, the national association allocates regional staff in different ways across the country, such that the number of national staff in each state and their relationship with the local affiliates vary.

In the first pair, both Greenville and Clinton center their activity around the most populous city in the state, which also happens to be the state capitol in the low-engagement state (but not in the high-engagement state). Both state affiliates have physical offices, where volunteer leaders, state staff, and national staff work alongside each other. Greenville has one additional staff person at the state level relative to Clinton, but they have the same number of national staff in their states. In Greenville, the state leaders and national organizers work relatively collaboratively with each other. In Clinton, they are cordial but relatively independent of each other. Clinton has four more local affiliates in its state than the high-engagement state. In both states, the elected leaders at the state level organize their work through committees, and Clinton has nine more

committees than Greenville. Programming in both states includes everything from social events designed to attract new members to political lobbying activity at the state, local, and national levels.

Both Springfield and Bristol have physical offices, but Bristol has one
more physical office in the state than Springfield. Both states have offices
in the state capitol, and these offices are shared by volunteer leaders, and
state and national staff. Both states have a paid staff person to coordinate
work at the state level. Springfield has two additional staff at the state level
relative to Bristol, but Bristol has more national staff than Springfield.
Bristol has two more local affiliates than Springfield. Both states have robust advocacy work going on at the state and local levels, and they both
integrate their work with the national staff working in their state.

In the third pair of states, the low-engagement state Salem had one
additional part-time staff person relative to Franklin, and one additional
part-time national staff organizer. Both states had physical offices located
in the state capitol and the same number of local affiliates in the state.
Salem had one additional committee at the state level relative to Franklin.
In both states, the national organizers and state and local leaders seemed
to work relatively independently of each other, even though their working
relationship was very friendly. Activities in both states were very similar
to each other, but the high-engagement state tended to have more social
events than the low-engagement states.

DATA COLLECTION FOR THE COMPARATIVE CASE STUDIES

To complement the explanations in chapters 1 and 2, I describe here the
kind of data I collected more fully. Within each local chapter, I conducted
a longitudinal study of member behavior and organizational actions.
Studying the process longitudinally allows me to compare people who
start in the same place, but take divergent paths. Some people choose to
take further actions, others do not. What led to one group taking one
path and the other group taking a different path? The study began by
gathering data on a group of members who had just joined a civic association. These new members completed an in-depth survey that captured

Table A-1. PROFILE OF NEW MEMBERS IN THE NATIONAL ASSOCIATION OF DOCTORS

Characteristic	Value
Professional status	
% Completed training, now a practicing physician	54.3
% In training (medical students, fellows, residents)	40.0
Gender: % Female	51.4
Mean age	41.5
Family status	
% Married	54.2
% With children	29.0
Mean years living in present town	11.4
Race	
% White	65.3
% Asian/Pacific Islander	26.4
% Black/African American	5.6
% Hispanic/Latino	2.8
2009 Household income	
% Under $100,000	42.3
% $100,000–199,999	26.8
% Over $200,000	31.0
Practice area	
Family practice/primary care	24.2
General internal medicine	16.1
Psychiatry	11.3
Pediatrics	9.7
Voting	
% Voting in "all elections"	66.7
% Voting in "most elections"	26.4
Political interest	
% "Extremely" or "fairly interested" in "politics and current affairs"	86.1
Political efficacy	
% "Someone like [me]" can have "a lot" of influence	9.7
% "Someone like [me]" can have "some" influence	66.7
Political ideology/partisanship	
% Liberal or extremely Liberal	70.8
% Democrat or strong Democrat	69.5

(Continued)

Table A-1 (Continued)

Characteristic	Value
% Engaging in the following activities "occasionally" or "often"	
Discussing politics	98.6
Signing written or email petitions	83.3
Buy products to support companies with certain social/ political values	72.2
Donating money to political candidates or causes	72.2
Boycotting products to oppose companies with certain social/political values	61.1
Working with others to solve problems in your community	59.7
Contacting public officials	50.0
Attending speeches, seminars, or teach-ins about politics	47.2
Displaying campaign buttons, stickers, or signs	45.8
Working or volunteering on an electoral campaign	29.2
Contacting newspapers or magazines	24.0
Participating in a protest, march, or demonstration	18.1
Calling in to radio/TV shows	7.0
Membership in civic groups	
% Belonging to 1–3 other civic organizations	61.1
% Belonging to 4 or more other civic organizations	20.8
Leadership and activity in civic organizations	
% Holding at least one leadership role in a civic organization	36.4
% Devoting no hours per month to civic organizations	27.8
% Devoting 1–5 hours per month to civic organizations	59.7
% Devoting 5 or more hours per month to civic organizations	12.5

baseline information about their involvement, including their current and past levels of civic and political participation, their initial reasons for becoming involved in the civic association, their current experiences with the association, demographics, including gender, age, race, household income, education level, partisanship, employment status, and so on. Subsequent to the initial survey, I tracked these members' involvement with the association using tools that already existed. The associations maintain data on their contact with members and the ways in which the members respond. Using these data, I was able to see if and when new members got involved. At the end of one year, I asked these individuals to complete another survey describing their involvement over the course of the year.

In addition to observing new members, I conducted in-depth interviews with association leaders and observations of association activity. I probed leaders about the logic behind the strategies they use, to juxtapose what the members experience with the intentions of the groups. Interview questions explored aggregate patterns of participation and involvement within the association; sources of variation in participation, from the subject's perspective; a description of strategies used to mobilize and make contact with members; and association considerations taken into account when choosing different strategies for mobilization. When possible, the interviews were conducted in person. Other interviews were conducted over the phone or via online video-conferencing tools like Skype.

Lastly, I conducted ethnographic observations of association activities, meetings, and events. Whenever possible, I visited each site in person to meet people face to face and observe their activity. When necessary, I introduced myself as a researcher studying the association to explain why I was sitting in on their events.

PROFILE OF NEW MEMBERS

National Association of Doctors

Table A-1 shows some basic demographic data on people joining the National Association of Doctors, using survey data collected in the longitudinal study. Approximately 54 percent of the sample were practicing physicians, while about 40 percent were in some stage of training, whether it be medical school, residency, or fellowship. For those who had chosen a specialty, 26 percent were in family practice or primary care, 16 percent in internal medicine, 11 percent in psychiatry, and just under 10 percent in pediatrics. Beyond that, respondents were divided into additional specialties. The sample is 51 percent female and the average age of respondents is 41 years. Just over half (54 percent) of the sample is married, but only 29 percent report having children. Respondents have, on average, lived in their present town for 11 years. About three-fifths (58 percent) of the sample has a general household income that tops $100,000 a year, with 22.5 percent of the sample making more than $250,000 a year.

Relative to the broader population of physicians in the United States, this sample overrepresents primary care physicians, women, and whites and Asians. Data from the American Medical Association (AMA) in 2006 shows that 56 percent of all physicians were white, while 12 percent were Asian.[29] These numbers are lower than the numbers reported in my sample above, but it is important to note that 22 percent of physicians in the AMA study had unknown racial backgrounds. The percentages of African American and Hispanic physicians in the sample are comparable to the numbers reported by the AMA. Women, however, join National Association of Doctors at rates disproportionate to their representation in the general population of physicians. According to the AMA, 28 percent of physicians in 2006 were female. The overrepresentation of women in National Association of Doctors is noteworthy, as Gruen, Campbell, and Blumenthal do not find that female doctors are necessarily more likely than male doctors to get involved in their communities or to rate community involvement as important.[30] They do find, however, that female doctors are 7 percentage points more likely to have gotten involved in politics than their male counterparts. Given the political nature of the association, it is possible that I am detecting the same trend here.

As shown in table A-1 the physicians and medical students who join National Association of Doctors are generally much more engaged in politics than the general population. Two-thirds of respondents report voting in all elections. Previous research shows that people routinely over-report their voting habits in survey data, but even accounting for that, this is still a relatively high rate of participation in elections. Similarly, 38 percent

29. Physician Characteristics and Distribution in the US, 2008, American Medical Association.

30. Gruen, Campbell, and Blumenthal 2006.

of respondents report being "extremely interested" in politics and current events, and 49 percent report being "fairly interested." Despite this strong self-report interest and participation in politics, respondents do not necessarily believe they have as much say in what government does. Only 10 percent of respondents believe they have "a lot" of influence over government decisions, but two-thirds believe they have "some" influence. This result appears to be slightly higher than the general population, in which 49 percent of the respondents to the American National Election Study agreed in 2008 that "people like me don't have any say about what government does." Finally, this group of respondents is far more politically progressive than the general population, which is not surprising given the progressive nature of National Association of Doctors.

These relatively high levels of participation and interest translate into participation in various kinds of political activity. Respondents are most likely to report being active in relatively low-risk activities that do not require a tremendous amount of time, although significant numbers of respondents are likely to report engaging in other, more time-consuming activities. This group of respondents is, in short, far more active than the general population. In the 2008 American National Elections Study (ANES), for example, only 13 percent of respondents reported donating money to a campaign, compared to 72 percent of respondents in this study. One-fifth (18 percent) of respondents in the ANES report displaying a campaign button, sticker, or sign, compared to 46 percent of the respondents in this study. Similarly, 4 percent of respondents in the ANES report volunteering for a campaign, while 29 percent of respondents in National Association of Doctors did.

These high rates of activity also translate into participation in civic groups. Fully 82 percent of respondents report being members of at least one other civic association in addition to National Association of Doctors, and 20 percent report being affiliated with five or more associations. For many respondents, participation goes further. Three-fourths of respondents report being active in at least one civic association (including National Association of Doctors) and 36 percent report being a leader in at least one civic association (note that none of the respondents are leaders

Table A-2. PROFILE OF NEW MEMBERS IN PEOPLE FOR THE ENVIRONMENT

Characteristic	Value
Gender: % Female	57.5
Mean age	53.5
Family status	
% Married	48.0
% with children	19.0
Race: % White	91.0
2009 Household income	
% Under $75,000	54.0
% $75,000–150,000	32.0
Education: % with post-graduate education	49.0
Work status	
% Working full-time	41.0
% Working part-time	10.0
% Retired	27.0
% Voting "often"	86.1
Political interest	
% "Extremely" or "fairly interested" in "politics and current affairs"	77.1
Political efficacy	
% "Someone like [me]" can have "a lot" of influence	6.1
% "Someone like [me]" can have "some" influence	43.9
Political ideology/partisanship	
% Liberal or extremely Liberal	70.8
% Democrat or strong Democrat	69.5
% Engaging in the following activities "occasionally" or "often"	
Discussing politics	94.6
Signing written or email petitions	73.4
Buy products to support companies with certain social/political values	68.5
Donating money to political candidates or causes	61.9
Working with others to solve problems in your community	49.4
Contacting public officials	48.6
Displaying campaign buttons, stickers, or signs	46.7
Attending speeches, seminars, or teach-ins about politics	36.2
Working or volunteering on an electoral campaign	25.6

(Continued)

Table A-2 (Continued)

Characteristic	Value
Contacting newspapers or magazines	21.5
Participating in a protest, march, or demonstration	19.4
Calling in to radio/TV shows	7.0
Membership in civic groups	
% Belonging to 1–2 other organizations	36.0
% Belonging to more than 2 other organizations	37.0
Leadership and activity in civic organizations	
% "Actively involved" in no groups	22.1
% "Actively involved" in 1 group	17.0
% "Actively involved" in 2 groups	19.0
% "Actively involved" in 3 groups	19.0

in National Association of Doctors). Despite these high rates of participation, most of this participation does not appear to be very time-consuming. Three-fifths (60 percent) of respondents report spending 1 to 5 hours per month with civic associations, and 11 percent report spending more than 5 hours per month. Given that 36 percent of respondents report being a leader in at least one association, but many fewer than that report spending more than five hours per month on associational activity, many of the leadership positions appear to not be very time-consuming.

People for the Environment

Table A-2 shows some basic demographic data about new members in People for the Environment using survey data from my longitudinal study. The average age of the new members was 53.5, and 57.5 percent of the sample was female. Just under half (48 percent) of the sample is married, and 81 percent of the sample has no children. The sample is 91 percent white, and 49 percent have some graduate education. Fifty-four percent of the sample makes $75,000 or less, and 86 percent of the sample makes $150,000 or less. Only 41 percent of the sample reports working full-time, with 10 percent of the sample working part-time and 27 percent of the sample being retired.

Compared to the general US population, this group of new members is older, whiter, more female, better educated, less likely to be working, and less likely to have children. In the United States overall, the 2010 Census found that 72.4 percent of the population was white, compared to 91 percent of those joining People for the Environment. The American Community Survey (ACS) estimates that women are 51 percent of the overall population, and the median age in the United States is 36.5 years. The ACS also estimates that only 10 percent of the US population aged 25 and over has a graduate degree, and that 65 percent of the population aged 16 years and over is in the labor force. Fifty percent of the population aged 15 and over is estimated to be married. Across the United States, 67 percent of households are estimated to make less than $75,000 a year, with 91 percent making less than $150,000 per year.[31] This profile of better educated, white members is consistent with previous research that finds the environmental movement tends to be comprised primarily of neo-liberal, white, wealthy, and well-educated individuals (Shaiko 1999). In addition, previous research has found that People for the Environment tends to have an older base of supporters than other segments of the environmental movement.

Table A-2 also shows data on the political orientation of new members to People for the Environment. The data show that people joining People for the Environment are far more politically engaged and progressive than the national population. Given that rates of participation in presidential elections hovers around 60 percent, and half of Americans cannot name the vice President in national surveys,[32] these data paint a picture of a highly engaged sample. Like the doctors joining National Association of Doctors, however, these high levels of engagement do not necessarily translate into high levels of efficacy. Only 6 percent of respondents feel like they have "a lot" of influence over government decisions, and 12 percent say they have "none." These numbers are relatively comparable to those reported in the general population, where 46 percent of respondents

31. All statistics from the U.S. Census Bureaus' American Fact Finder webpage. The data is drawn from the American Community Survey, 2005–2009. http://factfinder.census.gov/servlet/ACSSAFFPeople?_submenuId=people_0&_sse=on.

32. Patterson 2002.

self-identify as "Democrats" or "strong Democrats" and 49 percent identify as "liberal" or "extremely liberal." Although these levels are lower
than the percentage of new members in National Association of Doctors
self-identifying as progressives, they are still higher than the general
population.

These high levels of engagement correspond to relatively high levels of
participation in different kinds of civic and political activity. Almost all
of the respondents (95 percent) discuss political problems with others,
and some 62 percent of respondents report having donated money to a
political candidate or cause. More intensive forms of participation—such
as volunteering for campaigns, attending speeches, teach-ins, or seminars
about politics, and attending rallies or protests—draw fewer participants,
but are nonetheless still well-represented. Almost a quarter of respondents in this survey report volunteering for a political campaign, for example, compared to the 4 percent of respondents in the 2008 American
National Elections Study. Interestingly, only 22 percent of respondents
report contacting a newspaper or magazine and only 7 percent report
calling in to a radio or TV show. Respondents are much more likely to
take the time to contact public officials, in other words, than they are to
contact media. All these rates of participation are much higher than those
reported in the general population.

Members of People for the Environment are also very likely to be affiliated with other civic associations, including arts groups, social clubs,
sports leagues, recreational groups, religious associations, charity or
public service groups, and political parties or advocacy associations. If
we examine only the groups that are politically oriented (excluding recreational groups, religious organizations, and charity or public service
organizations), 36 percent of respondents affiliate with one or two of these
groups, 37 percent affiliate with more than two such groups. Many of the
groups with which people are affiliated, in other words, are nonpoliti-
cal organizations. Further, we find that many people are only minimally
involved in these groups. Some 22 percent of people say they are not actively involved in any of the groups, and 17 percent say they are active in
just one group. Nineteen percent of people say they are actively involved
in two groups, and 19 percent say three groups.

Aldrich, John. 1997. Positive Theory and Voice and Equality. *American Political Science Review* 91 (2): 421–423.

Andrews, Kenneth T., and Bob Edwards. 2004. Advocacy Organizations in the U.S. Political Process. *Annual Review of Sociology* 30: 479–506.

Andrews, Kenneth T., Marshall Ganz, Matthew Baggetta, Hahrie Han, and Chaeyoon Lim. 2010. Leadership, Membership, and Voice: Civic Associations That Work. *American Journal of Sociology* 115 (4): 1191–1242.

Ansolabehere, Stephen, and Shanto Iyengar. 1995. *Going Negative: How Political Advertisements Shrink and Polarize the Electorate*. New York: Simon and Schuster.

Arceneaux, Kevin. 2007. I'm Asking for Your Support: The Effects of Personally Delivered Campaign Messages on Voting Decisions and Opinion Formation. *Quarterly Journal of Political Science* 2 (1): 43–65.

Baggetta, Matthew, Hahrie Han, and Kenneth T. Andrews. 2013. Leading Associations: How Individual Characteristics and Team Dynamics Generate Committed Leaders. *American Sociological Review* 78 (4): 544–573.

Bandura, Albert. 1997. *Self-Efficacy: The Exercise of Control*. New York: W. H. Freeman and Company.

Barakso, Maryann. 2004. *Governing Now: Grassroots Activism in the National Organization for Women*. Ithaca, NY: Cornell University Press.

Baumgartner, Frank, and Beth Leech. 1998. *Basic Interests*. Princeton, NJ: Princeton University Press.

Baumgartner, Frank, Jeffrey M. Berry, Marie Hojnacki, David C. Kimball, and Beth L. Leech. 2009. *Lobbying and Policy Change: Who Wins, Who Loses, and Why*. Chicago: University of Chicago Press.

Bennett, Lance. 2012. The Personalization of Politics: Political Identity, Social Media, and Changing Patterns of Participation. *The ANNALS of the American Academy of Political and Social Science* 644: 20–39.

Berry, Jeffrey M. 1999. *The New Liberalism: The Rising Power of Citizen Groups*. Washington, DC: Brookings Institution Press.

Beyerlein, Kraig, and John Hipp. 2006. A Two-Stage Model for a Two-Stage Process: How Biographical Availability Matters for Social Movement Mobilization. *Mobilization* 11: 219–240.

Bimber, Bruce. 2003. *Information and American Democracy: Technology in the Evolution of Political Power.* New York: Cambridge University Press.

Bimber, Bruce, Andrew Flanagin, and Cynthia Stohl. 2012. *Collective Action in Organizations: Interaction and Engagement in an Era of Technological Change.* New York: Cambridge University Press.

Blau, Peter M. 1970. A Formal Theory of Differentiation in Organizations. *American Sociological Review* 35: 201–218.

Brader, Ted. 2006. *Campaigning for Hearts and Minds: How Emotional Appeals in Political Ads Work.* Chicago: University of Chicago Press.

Brady, David W., and Pietro S. Nivola. 2007. *Red and Blue Nation? Consequences and Corrections of America's Polarized Politics.* Vol. 2. Washington, DC: Brookings Institution Press and Hoover Institution.

Brady, Henry E. 1999. Political Participation. In *Measures of Political Attitudes, Measures of Social Psychological Attitudes*, edited by J. P. Robinson, P. R. Shaver, and L. S. Wrightsman, 737–801. New York: Academic Press.

Burger, J. M., S. Soroka, K. Gonzago, E. Murphy, and E. Somervell. 2001. The Effect of Fleeting Attraction on Compliance to Requests. *Personality and Social Psychology Bulletin* 27: 1578–1586.

Canes-Wrone, Brandice, David W. Brady, and John F. Cogan. 2002. Out of Step, Out of Office: Electoral Accountability and House Members' Voting. *American Political Science Review* 96 (1): 127–140.

Christens, Brian, Paul Speer, and N. Andrew Peterson. 2011. Social Class as Moderator of the Relationship between (Dis)Empowering Processes and Psychological Empowerment. *Journal of Community Psychology* 39 (2): 170–182.

Cialdini, Robert B. 2001. *Influence, Science and Practice.* 4th ed. Needham Heights, MA: Allyn and Bacon.

Cialdini, Robert B., and Noah J. Goldstein. 2004. Social Influence: Compliance and Conformity. *Annual Review of Psychology* 55: 591–621.

Clemens, Elisabeth. 1997. *The People's Lobby.* Chicago: University of Chicago Press.

Corrigall-Brown, Catherine. 2012. *Patterns of Protest: Trajectories of Participation in Social Movements.* Stanford, CA: Stanford University Press.

Damasio, Antonio R. 1994. *Descartes' Error: Emotion, Reason, and the Human Brain.* New York: Grosset/Putnam Books.

Diamond, Sara. 1998. *Not by Politics Alone.* New York: Guilford Press.

Dolinski, D., M. Nawrat, and I. Rudak. 2001. Dialogue Involvement as a Social Influence Technique. *Personality and Social Psychology Bulletin* 27: 1395–1406.

Dorius, Cassandra, and John D. McCarthy. 2009. *The Role of Gender, Grievance and Bureaucratic Complexity in Explaining Leadership Effort in the Early Stages of the Movement Against Drunk Driving.* University Park, PA: Pennsylvania State University.

Dorius, Cassandra R., and John D. McCarthy. 2011. Understanding Activist Leadership Effort in the Movement Opposing Drinking and Driving. *Social Forces* 90: 453–473.

Ehrhardt-Martinez, Karen, and John A. Laitner, eds. 2010. *People-Centered Initiatives for Increasing Energy Savings*. Washington, DC: American Council for an Energy-Efficient Economy.

Eliasoph, Nina. 2011. *Making Volunteers: Civic Life after Welfare's End*. Princeton, NJ: Princeton University Press.

Erikson, Robert S., Michael B. MacKuen, and James Stimson. 2002. *The Macro Polity*. New York: Cambridge University Press.

Fiorina, Morris P. 2003. Parties, Participation, and Representation in America: Old Theories Face New Realities. In *Political Science: The State of the Discipline*, edited by I. Katznelson and H. Milner, 511–541. New York: W. W. Norton & Co.

Fung, Archon. 2003. Associations and Democracy: Between Theories, Hopes, and Realities. *Annual Review of Sociology* 29: 515–539.

Fung, Archon, and Jennifer Shkabatur. 2012. *Viral Engagement: Fast, Cheap, and Broad, but Good for Democracy?* Unpublished manuscript. Cambridge, MA: Harvard University.

Gamson, William A. 1992. *Talking Politics*. New York: Cambridge University Press.

Ganz, Marshall. 2001. The Power of Story in Social Movements. Paper read at Annual Meeting of the American Sociological Association, August, at Anaheim, California.

——. 2009. *Why David Sometimes Wins: Leadership, Strategy and the Organization in the California Farm Worker Movement*. New York: Oxford University Press.

——. 2010. Leading Change: Leadership, Organization, and Social Movements. In *Handbook of Leadership Theory and Practice*, edited by N. Nohria and R. Khurana, 1–42. Cambridge, MA: Harvard Business School Press.

Garcia-Bedolla, Lisa, and Melissa R. Michelson. 2012. *Mobilizing Inclusion: Transforming the Electorate through Get-Out-the-Vote Campaigns* New Haven, CT: Yale University Press.

Geer, John G. 2006. *In Defense of Negativity: Attack Advertising in Presidential Campaigns*. Chicago: University of Chicago Press.

Gerber, Alan S., and Donald P. Green. 2000. The Effects of Canvassing, Telephone Calls, and Direct Mail on Voter Turnout: A Field Experiment. *American Political Science Review* 94 (3): 653–663.

Gerber, Alan, Donald Green, and Christopher Larimer. 2008. Social Pressure and Voter Turnout: Evidence from a Large-Scale Field Experiment. *American Political Science Review* 102 (1): 33–48.

Gladwell, Malcolm. 2010. Small Change: Why the Revolution Will Not be Tweeted. *New Yorker*, October 4.

Green, Donald, and Alan Gerber. 2004. *Get Out the Vote!: A Guide for Candidates and Campaigns*. New Haven, CT: Yale University Press.

——. 2008. *Get Out the Vote: How to Increase Voter Turnout*. Washington, DC: The Brookings Institution.

Gruen, Russel L., Eric G. Campbell, and David Blumenthal. 2006. Public Roles of US Physicians: Community Participation, Political Involvement, and Collective Advocacy. *Journal of the American Medical Association* 296 (20): 2467–2475.

Hacker, Jacob S., and Paul Pierson. 2010. *Winner-Take-All Politics: How Washington Made the Rich Richer—and Turned Its Back on the Middle Class*. New York: Simon and Schuster.

Hackman, Richard. 2002. *Leading Teams: Setting the State for Great Performances*. New York: Harvard Business School.

Hall, Bob, and Mary Lee Kerr. 1991. *The Green Index: A State by State Guide to the Nation's Environmental Health*. Washington, DC: Island Press.

Han, Hahrie. 2009. *Moved to Action: Motivation, Participation, and Inequality in American Politics*. Palo Alto, CA: Stanford University Press.

——. 2014. "Experiments of Identity-Based Approaches to Cultivating Activism." Unpublished manuscript. Wellesley, MA: Wellesley College.

Han, Hahrie, and David W. Brady. 2007. A Delayed Return to Historical Norms: Congressional Party Polarization after the Second World War. *British Journal of Political Science* 37 (3): 505–531.

Hansen, John Mark. 1991. *Gaining Access: Congress and the Farm Lobby, 1919–1981*. Chicago: University of Chicago Press.

Hetherington, Marc. 2005. *Why Trust Matters: Declining Political Trust and the Demise of American Liberalism*. Princeton, NJ: Princeton University Press.

Hibbing, John R., and Elizabeth Theiss-Morse. 2001. *What is it about Government that Americans Dislike?* Cambridge Studies in Public Opinion and Political Psychology. New York: Cambridge University Press.

Hillygus, Sunshine, and Todd Shields. 2008. *The Persuadable Voter: Wedge Issues in Presidential Campaigns*. Princeton, NJ: Princeton University Press.

Hutchings, Vincent L. 2003. *Public Opinion and Democratic Accountability: How Citizens Learn about Politics*. Princeton, NJ: Princeton University Press.

Issenberg, Sasha. 2012. *The Victory Lab: The Secret Science of Winning Campaigns*. New York: Crown.

Jacobs, Lawrence R., and Theda Skocpol. 2010. *Health Care Reform and American Politics: What Everyone Needs to Know*. New York: Oxford University Press.

Jennings, M. Kent. 1987. Residues of a Movement: The Aging of the American Protest Generation. *American Political Science Review* 81 (2): 367–382.

Kanter, Rosabeth Moss. 1972. *Commitment and Community*. Cambridge, MA: Harvard University Press.

Karpf, David. 2012. *The MoveOn Effect: The Unexpected Transformation of American Political Advocacy*. New York: Oxford University Press.

Klandermans, Bert. 2007. The Demand and Supply of Participation : Social-Psychological Correlates of Participation in Social Movements. In *The Blackwell Companion to Social Movements*, edited by D. A. Snow, S. A. Soule, and H. Kriesi, 360–379. Malden, MA: Blackwell Publishing.

Klandermans, Bert, and Dirk Oegema. 1987. Potentials, Networks, Motivations, and Barriers: Steps Towards Participation in Social Movements. *American Sociological Review* 52: 519–531.

Klein, Howard J., Thomas E. Becker, and John P. Meyer, eds. 2009. *Commitment in Organizations: Accumulated Wisdom and New Directions*. New York: Routledge Academic.

Knoke, David. 1986. Associations and Interest Groups. *Annual Review of Sociology* 12: 1–21.

Kreiss, Daniel. 2012. *Taking Our Country Back: The Crafting of Network Politics from Howard Dean to Barack Obama*. New York: Oxford University Press.

Landers, S. H., and A. R. Sehgal. 2000. How Do Physicians Lobby Their Members of Congress? *Archives of Internal Medicine* 160: 3248–3251.

Lesage, Julia. 1998. Christian Coalition Leadership Training. In *Culture, Media, and the Religious Right*, edited by Julia Lesage and L. Kintz, 295–326. Minneapolis: University of Minnesota Press.

Marcus, George E. 2002. *The Sentimental Citizen: Emotion in Democratic Politics*. University Park: Pennsylvania State University Press.

Marcus, George E., W. Russell Neuman, and Michael B. MacKuen. 2000. *Affective Intelligence and Political Judgment*. Chicago: University of Chicago Press.

McAdam, Doug. 1989. The Biographical Consequences of Activism. *American Sociological Review* 54 (5): 744–760.

McAdam, Doug, Sidney Tarrow, and Charles Tilly, eds. 2001. *Dynamics of Contention*. New York: Cambridge University Press.

McKenna, Elizabeth, and Hahrie Han. 2014. *Groundbreakers: How Obama's 2.2 Millions Volunteers Transformed Campaigns in America*. New York: Oxford University Press.

Mele, Nicco. 2013. *The End of Big: How the Internet Makes David the New Goliath*. New York: St. Martin's Press.

Miller, Joanne M. 2005. Why Do Individuals Participate in Politics? Paper read at Annual Meeting of the Midwest Political Science Association, at Chicago, IL.

Morozov, Evgeny. 2009. The Brave New World of Slacktivism. *Foreign Policy*, May 19.

Morris, Aldon, and Suzanne Staggeborg. 2007. Leadership in Social Movements. In *The Blackwell Companion to Social Movements*, edited by D. A. Snow, S. A. Soule, and H. Kriesi, 171–196. New York: Wiley-Blackwell.

Munson, Ziad. 2009. *The Making of Pro-life Activists: How Social Movement Mobilization Works*. Chicago: University of Chicago Press.

Murray, Peter. 2013. The Secret of Scale: How Powerful Civic Organizations like the NRA and AARP Build Membership, Make Money, and Sway Public Policy. *Stanford Social Innovation Review*, 32–39.

Musick, Marc A., and John Wilson. 2008. *Volunteers: A Social Profile*. Bloomington and Indianapolis: Indiana University Press.

Mutz, Diana. 2006. *Hearing the Other Side: Deliberative versus Participatory Democracy*. Cambridge: Cambridge University Press.

Nickerson, David. 2006. Volunteer Phone Calls Can Increase Turnout. *American Politics Research* 34 (3): 271–292.

———. 2008. Is Voting Contagious? Evidence from Two Field Experiments. *American Political Science Review* 102 (February): 49–57.

Nussbaum, Martha C. 2001. *Upheavals of Thought: The Intelligence of Emotions*. New York: Cambridge University Press.

Olson, Mancur. 1965. *The Logic of Collective Action: Public Goods and the Theory of Groups*. Cambridge, MA: Harvard University Press.

Orum, Anthony, and John Dale. 2009. *Political Sociology, Power and Participation in the Modern World*. 5th ed. New York: Oxford University Press.

Pastor, Manuel, Jennifer Ito, and Rachel Rosner. 2011. *Metrics that Matter for Building, Scaling, and Funding Social Movements*. Los Angeles: USC Program for Environmental and Regional Equity.

Patterson, Thomas E. 2002. *The Vanishing Voter: Public Involvement in an Age of Uncertainty*. New York: Alfred A. Knopf.

Plutzer, Eric. 2002. Becoming a Habitual Voter: Inertia, Resources, and Growth in Young Adulthood. *American Political Science Review* 96 (1): 41–56.

Polletta, Francesca. 2006. *It Was Like a Fever: Storytelling in Protest and Politics*. Chicago: University of Chicago Press.

Polletta, Francesca, and James M. Jasper. 2001. Collective Identity and Social Movements. *Annual Review of Sociology* 27: 283–305.

Putnam, Robert. 1995. Bowling Alone: America's Declining Social Capital. *Journal of Democracy* 6 (1): 65–78.

——. 2001. *Bowling Alone: The Collapse and Revival of American Democracy*. New York: Simon and Schuster.

Quadagno, Jill S. 2006. *One Nation, Uninsured: Why the U.S. Has No National Health Insurance*. New York: Oxford University Press.

Robnett, Belinda. 1996. African-American Women in the Civil Rights Movement, 1954–1965: Gender, Leadership, and Micromobilization. *American Journal of Sociology* 101 (6): 1661–1693.

Rogers, Todd, Alan S. Gerber, and Craig R. Fox. 2012. Rethinking Why People Vote: Voting as Dynamic Social Expression. In *Behavioral Foundations of Policy*, edited by E. Shafir, 91–107. Princeton, NJ: Princeton University Press.

Rosenstone, Steven J., and John Mark Hansen. 1993. *Mobilization, Participation, and Democracy in America*. New York: Macmillan Publishing Company.

Rothenberg, Lawrence. 1992. *Linking Citizens to Government: Interest Group Politics at Common Cause*. New York: Cambridge University Press.

Sampson, Robert, J. Morenoff, and T. Gannon-Rowley. 2002. Assessing Neighborhood Effects: Social Processes and New Directions in Research. *Annual Review of Sociology* 28: 443–478.

Schier, Steven. 2000. *By Invitation Only: The Rise of Exclusive Politics in the United States*. Pittsburgh: University of Pittsburgh Press.

Schlozman, Kay Lehman. 2003. Citizen Participation in America: What Do We Know? Why Do We Care? In *Political Science, State of the Discipline*, edited by I. Katznelson and H. Milner, 433–461. New York: W. W. Norton and Company.

Schlozman, Kay Lehman, and John C. Tierney. 1986. *Organized Interests and American Democracy*. New York: Harper and Row.

Schlozman, Kay Lehman, Sidney Verba, and Henry Brady. 2012. *The Unheavenly Chorus: Unequal Political Voice and the Broken Promise of American Democracy*. New York: Princeton University Press.

Schussman, Alan, and Sarah A. Soule. 2005. Process and Protest: Accounting for Individual Protest Participation. *Social Forces* 84: 1084–1108.

Shaiko, Ronald. 1999. *Voices and Echoes for the Environment: Public Interest Representation in the 1990s and Beyond*. New York: Columbia University Press.

Skocpol, Theda. 2003. *Diminished Democracy: From Membership to Management in American Civic Life*. Norman: University of Oklahoma Press.

——. 2013. *Naming the Problem: What It Will Take to Counter Extremism and Engage Americans in the Fight against Global Warming*. Cambridge, MA: Harvard University Press.

Skocpol, Theda, Marshall Ganz, and Ziad Munson. 2000. A Nation of Organizers: The Institutional Origins of Civic Voluntarism in the United States. *American Political Science Review* 94 (3): 527–546.

Smith, Jonathan E., Kenneth P. Carson, and Ralph A. Alexander. 1984. Leadership: It Can Make a Difference. *Academy of Management Journal* 27 (4): 765–776.

Smith, Richard. 1995. Interest Group Influence in the U.S. Congress. *Legislative Studies Quarterly* 20: 89–139.

Smock, Kristina. 2004. *Democracy in Action: Community Organizing and Urban Change*. New York: Columbia University Press.

Snow, David A. 2001. Collective Identity and Expressive Forms. In *International Encyclopedia of the Social and Behavioral Sciences*, edited by N. Smelser and P. D. Baltes, 2212–2219. Oxford, UK: Pergamon Press.

——. 2007. Framing Processes, Ideology, and Discursive Fields. In *The Blackwell Companion to Social Movements*, edited by D. A. Snow, S. A. Soule, and H. Kriesi, 380–412. Malden, MA: Blackwell Publishing.

Snow, David A., and Robert D. Benford. 1988. Ideology, Frame Resonance, and Participant Mobilization. *International Social Movement Research* 1: 197–217.

Snow, David, and Sarah Soule. 2010. *A Primer on Social Movements*. New York: W. W. Norton.

Snow, David A., Sarah A. Soule, and Hanspeter Kriesi. 2007. *The Blackwell Companion to Social Movements*. New York: Wiley-Blackwell.

Speer, Paul, and Brian Christens. 2011. Contextual Influences on Participation in Community Organizing. *American Journal of Community Psychology* 47 (44): 253–263.

Speer, Paul W., N. Andrew Peterson, Allison Zippay, and Brian D Christens. 2010. Participation in Congregation-Based Community Organizing: Mixed-Method Study of Civic Engagement. In *Using Evidence to Inform Practice for Community and Organizational Change*, edited by M. Roberts-Degennaro and S. J. Fogel, 200–217. Chicago, IL: Lyceum Books, Inc.

Stoker, Laura, and M. Kent Jennings. 1995. Life-Cycle Transitions and Political Participation: The Case of Marriage. *American Political Science Review* 89: 421–436.

Taylor, Verta, and Nella Van Dyke. 2007. "Get Up Stand Up": Tactical Repertoires of Social Movements. In *The Blackwell Companion to Social Movements*, edited by D. A. Snow, S. A. Soule, and H. Kriesi, 262–293. New York: Wiley-Blackwell.

Teske, Nathan. 1997a. Beyond Altruism: Identity-Construction as Moral Motive in Political Explanation. *Political Psychology* 18 (1): 71–91.

——. 1997b. *Political Activists in America: The Identity Construction Model of Political Participation*. New York: Cambridge University Press.

Tilly, Charles. 1978. *From Mobilization to Revolution*. Reading, MA: Addison-Wesley.

——. 1986. *The Contentious French*. Cambridge, MA: Harvard University Press.

Tocqueville, Alexis de. [1835–40] 1969. *Democracy in America*. New York: Harper Perennial.

Tufecki, Zeynep. 2014. Capabilities of Movements and Affordances of Digital Media: Paradoxes of Empowerment. In *dmlcentral.net*: Digital Media and Learning Research Hub.

US Department of Commerce, Census Bureau. 2009. Current Population Survey (2008–09). http://www.census.gov/cps/.

Van der Vegt, Gerben S., and Onne Janssen. 2003. Joint Impact of Interdependence and Group Diversity on Innovation. *Journal of Management* 29: 729–751.

Verba, Sidney, and Norman Nie. 1972. *Participation in America: Political Democracy and Social Equality.* New York: Harper and Row.

Verba, Sidney, Kay Lehman Schlozman, and Henry Brady. 1995. *Voice and Equality: Civic Voluntarism in American Politics.* Cambridge, MA: Harvard University Press.

Walker, Jack L., Jr. 1991. *Mobilizing Interest Groups in America: Patrons, Professions, and Social Movements.* Ann Arbor: University of Michigan Press.

Wandersman, Abraham, Paul Florin, Robert Friedmann, and Ron Meier. 1987. Who Participates, Who Does Not, and Why? An Analysis of Voluntary Neighborhood Organizations in the United States and Israel. *Sociological Forum* 2: 534–555.

Warren, Mark. 2001. *Dry Bones Rattling: Community Building to Revitalize American Democracy, Princeton Studies in American Politics.* Princeton, NJ: Princeton University Press.

Wilcox, Clyde. 2000. *Onward Christian Soldiers? The Religious Right in American Politics.* 2nd ed. Boulder, CO: Westview Press.

Wilson, James Q. 1973. *Political Organizations.* New York: Basic Books, Inc.

Wilson, John, and Marc A. Musick. 1999. Attachment to Volunteering. *Sociological Forum* 14: 243–272.

Wolfinger, Raymond E., and Steven J. Rosenstone. 1980. *Who Votes?* New Haven, CT: Yale University Press.

Zald, Mayer N., and John D. McCarthy. 1987. *Social Movements in an Organizational Society.* New Brunswick, NJ: Transaction Publishers.

Zeldin, Shepherd, and Dmitri Topitzes. 2002. Neighborhood Experiences, Community Connection, and Positive Beliefs about Adolescents among Urban Adults and Youth. *Journal of Community Psychology* 30: 647–669.

Figures, notes, and tables are indicated by "f," "n," and "t" following page numbers.

Printed in Poland
by Amazon Fulfillment
Poland Sp. z o.o., Wrocław